Collins

INTERNATIONAL PRIMARY ENGLISH

Teacher's Guide 1

An imprint of HarperCollinsPublishers
The News Building
1 London Bridge Street
London SE1 9GF

Browse the complete Collins catalogue at
www.collins.co.uk

British Library Cataloguing in Publication Data
A catalogue record for this publication is available from the British Library.

Publisher Celia Wigley
Publishing manager Karen Jamieson
Commissioning editor Lucy Cooper
Series editor Karen Morrison
Managing editor Caroline Green
Editor Amanda Redstone
Project managed by Emily Hooton and Karen Williams
Edited by Tasia Vassalatou
Proofread by Gaynor Spry
Cover design by Amparo Barrera
Cover artwork by Laura Hambleton
Internal design by Ken Vail Graphic Design
Typesetting by Ken Vail Graphic Design and Contentra Technologies India Private Limited
Illustrations by Ken Vail Graphic Design, Advocate Art and Beehive Illustrations
Production by Robin Forrester

Printed and bound by CPI Group (UK) Ltd, Croydon, CR0 4YY

Contents

Introduction

About Collins International Primary English

Collins International Primary English is specifically written to meet fully the requirements of the Cambridge International Examinations Primary English Framework, and the material has been carefully developed to meet the needs of primary English learners and teachers in a range of international contexts.

The material at each level has been organised into nine units, each based around particular text types. The activities in each unit are introduced and explored in contexts related to the selected texts.

The course materials are supplemented and enhanced by a range of print and electronic resources, including photocopiable (printable) master sheets for support, extension and assessment of classroom based activities (you can find these on pages 87 to 119 of this Teacher's Guide as well as on the digital resource) and a range of interactive digital activities to add interest and excitement to learning. Reading texts are supported by audio-visual presentations.

Components of the course

For each of Stages 1–6 as detailed in the Cambridge Primary English Framework, we offer:

- a full colour, highly illustrated Student's Book with integral reading texts
- a write-in Workbook linked to the Student's Book
- this comprehensive Teacher's Guide with clear instructions for using the materials
- an interactive digital package, which includes warm-up presentations, audio files of readings, interactive activities and record keeping for teacher use only.

Approach

The course is designed with learner-centred learning at its heart. Learners work through a range of contextualised reading, writing, speaking and listening activities with guidance and support from their teacher. Plenty of opportunity is provided for the learners to consolidate and apply what they have learnt and to relate what they are learning both to other contexts and the environment in which they live.

Much of the learners' work is conducted in pairs or small groups in line with international best practice. The tasks and activities are designed to be engaging for the learners and to support teachers in their assessment of learner progress and achievement. Each set of lessons is planned to support clear learning objectives and the activities within each unit provide opportunities for oral and written feedback by the teacher as well as self- and peer-assessment options.

Throughout the course, there is a wide variety of learning experiences on offer. The materials are organised so that they do not impose a rigid structure, but rather allow for a range of options linked to the learning objectives.

Differentiation

Differentiation in the form of support and extension ideas is built into the unit-by-unit teaching support in this Teacher's Guide.

Achievement levels are likely to vary from learner to learner, so we have included a graded set of assessment criteria in each weekly review section. The **square**, **circle** and **triangle** assessment criteria indicate what learners at varying levels might be expected to have achieved each week. The **square** indicates what can be expected of almost all learners. The **circle** indicates what might be expected of most learners, and the **triangle** indicates what level of achievement might be expected from more able learners. Levels will vary as some learners may find some topics more interesting and/or easier; similarly, some may excel at speaking activities rather than written ones.

Teacher's Guide

The Teacher's Guide offers detailed guidance for covering each unit. Each unit is designed to cover three teaching weeks. The teacher knows their class and context best, so they should feel free to vary the pace and the amount of work covered each week to suit their circumstances. Each unit has a clear structure, with an introduction, suggestions for introducing the unit, learning objectives and a resource list of supporting materials that can be used in the unit.

Student's Book

The Student's Book offers a clear structure and easy-to-follow design to help learners to navigate the course. The following features are found at all levels:

- A range of fiction, non-fiction, poetry, play scripts and transactional texts are provided to use as a starting point for contextualised learning.
- Skills-based headers allow teachers to locate activities within the curriculum framework and indicate to learners what skills are being focused on in each task.
- Clear instruction rubrics are provided for each activity. The rubrics allow learners to develop more and more independent learning as they begin to master and understand instructive text. The rubrics also model assessment type tasks and prepare them for formal assessment at all levels.
- Some text have audio-visual support on Collins Connect. Teachers can play these to the class and learners can use these themselves if they need to listen to the text again.
- Grammar and language boxes provide teaching text and examples to show the language feature in use. These are coloured so that learners can easily recognise them as they work through the course.
- The notepad feature contains reminders, hints and interesting facts.

Workbook

The Workbook is clearly linked to the Student's Book. The activities here contain structured spaces for the learners to record answers. The activities can be used as classroom tasks, for homework, or for assessment purposes. The completed Workbook tasks give the teacher an opportunity to check work and give written feedback and/or grades. The learners have a consolidated record of their work and parents or guardians can see what kind of activities the learners are doing in class.

Digital resources

The digital resources are offered online by subscription. You can access these at Collins Connect. These resources can be used to introduce topics and support learning and assessment. The unit guidelines in this Teacher's Guide offer suggestions for when and how to use these resources.

The interactive activities include:

- drag-and-drop activities
- matching activities
- look-cover-say-spell activities
- cloze procedure (fill in the missing words)
- labelling diagrams
- and many more.

Learners receive instant feedback when they complete the activities and the responses are randomised so the learners can complete the tasks they enjoy more than once, getting a different arrangement of items each time.

Some materials can be printed out for use in the classroom. For example, there is an additional assessment task provided for each unit. This is in the form of a simple test. It can be printed and used in class or as a homework task. These tasks are teacher marked. There is also a set of activity sheets which can be used for support, extension and homework as required.

Collins Connect offers an easy and accessible method of keeping records. Teachers can compile class lists and keep track of progress in an easy-to-use and well-supported system.

Assessment in primary English

In the Collins International Primary English course, assessment is a continuous, planned process that involves collecting information about learner progress and learning in order to provide constructive feedback to both learners and parents or guardians and also to guide planning and the next teaching steps.

Cambridge International Examinations Primary English Curriculum Framework makes it clear what the learners are expected to learn and achieve at each level. Our task as teachers is to assess whether or not the learners have achieved the stated goals using clearly-focused, varied, reliable and flexible methods of assessment.

In the Collins International Primary English course, assessment is continuous and in-built. It applies the principles of international best practice and ensures that assessment:

- is ongoing and regular
- supports individual achievement and allows for learners to reflect on their learning and set targets for themselves
- provides feedback and encouragement to the learners
- allows for integration of assessment into the activities and classroom teaching by

combining different assessment methods, including observations, questioning, self-assessment and formal and informal tasks/tests

- uses strategies that cater for a variety of learner needs in the classroom (language, physical, emotional and cultural), and acknowledges that the learners do not all need to be assessed at the same time, or in the same way
- allows for, and prepares learners for, more formal summative assessment including controlled activities, tasks and tests.

Formal written assessment

The Collins International Primary English course offers a set of assessment sheets that teachers can use to assess learning formally and to award marks if necessary. These sheets test the skills and competencies developed in a cumulative manner. In some cases, learners will use the same texts as context; in other cases; they will be expected to read and make sense of an unseen text and to answer a range of contextualised questions based on that.

At Stage 1, there is a short assessment task at the end of each unit.

In addition to the materials supplied in the course, schools may opt for their learners to take standardised Cambridge International Examinations progression tests at Stages 3, 4, 5 and 6. These tests are developed by Cambridge but they are written and marked in schools. Teachers download tests and administer them in their own classrooms. Cambridge International Examinations provides a mark scheme and you can upload learners' test results and then analyse the results and print reports. You can also compare a learner's results against their class, school or other schools around the world and on a year-by-year basis.

Laying the foundations of learning to read in the early stages

To learn to read and write, learners need to be phonologically aware and have a functional understanding of the alphabet along with an understanding of the purpose and value of print. Successful reading and writing depends on their ability to make the association between all three of these skills.

Learning to read should be treated as an enjoyable problem-solving activity. Learners must be encouraged to use a wide range of strategies to help them to read unknown words.

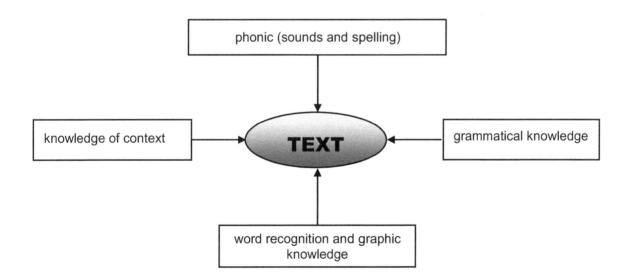

First 100 high frequency words

the	and	a	to	said
that	with	all	we	can
are	up	had	my	her
what	there	out	this	have
went	be	like	some	so
in	he	I	of	it
was	you	they	on	she
is	for	at	his	but
find	more	I'll	round	tree
magic	shouted	us	other	food
fox	through	way	been	stop
must	red	door	right	sea
these	began	boy	animals	never
next	first	work	lots	need
that's	baby	fish	gave	mouse
something	bed	may	still	found
live	say	soon	night	narrator
small	car	couldn't	three	head
king	town	I've	around	every
garden	fast	only	many	laughed

Phonics

Phonics is a strategy for teaching reading and spelling of the English language. It focuses on developing the learners' ability to hear, identify and manipulate phonemes, in order to teach the correspondence between these sounds and the spelling patterns that represent them. A phonics programme should foster a steady development of phonological and phonemic awareness.

Phonological awareness is an explicit awareness of the sounds in words, demonstrated by the ability to identify onset, generate rhyme and segment syllables in words.

The smallest unit of sound in a word is called a phoneme. There are approximately 44 phonemes in the English language. A phoneme can be formed by one, two, three or four letters. For example:

c as in 'cot' – one letter
ch as in 'chat' – two letters

–igh as in 'high' – three letters
–tion as in 'station' – four letters

'Cat' has three phonemes (c-a-t), but 'chat' also has three phonemes (ch-a-t).

The 44 sounds are represented by the 26 letters (graphemes) of the alphabet.

There are a number of skills that should be taught and practised in a phonic programme.

8

1 Letter sounds (phonemes)

Learning the letter sounds should include alphabet sounds as well as two letters making one sound, like *sh*, *ch*, *ng*. It should also include learning that the same sound can be represented in more than one way, such as as *ai*/*ay* representing the long vowel *a* and the same spelling can represent more than one sound, such as *ow* in 'now' and 'show'.

2 Letter formation

Learners should learn to form the letters correctly and consistently.

3 Blending

Learners should learn to blend sounds together to read a word. In order to read an unfamiliar word phonemically a learner must attribute a phoneme (sound) to each letter or letter combination in the word and then merge the phonemes together to pronounce the word.

4 Segmenting

Learners should learn to listen and break a word down into its component sounds, for example *c-a-t*, *sh-o-p*. Learners need to be able to do this to produce a written word (spelling) from a spoken word.

5 Onset and rime

Onset is the initial consonant or consonant cluster of letters (adjacent consonants) in words which precedes the vowel, for example '*b*ag', '*cl*ock'.

Rime refers to the vowel and final consonant(s). For example –*at* in 'cat', –*ing* in 'string' or the final digraph e.g. –*ow* in 'how', 'now', 'cow'.

When a learner is learning to read and write there are two crucial things to learn:

- the sounds represented by written letters
- how to blend the sounds together to make a word, and how to break a word into its component sounds (segments) to spell a word.

Alphabet sounds – Learners should be given opportunities to learn the relationship between letter (grapheme) and sound (phoneme) and to hear, read and write the alphabet sounds. At first the focus is on the sound that an alphabet letter represents but the learners should learn the names of each alphabet letter and the sound each represents. You should use the words 'name' and 'sound' correctly when speaking to the learners. It is very

important when teaching learners to learn the alphabet sounds to remember not to add an *uh* to the end of consonant sounds – so say *mmm* and not *muh*. It is then easier to blend the sounds together to make words. The focus in the beginning is on letters as initial sounds as in '*h*at' and '*p*at', but very quickly every opportunity must be taken to make learners aware that sounds appear at the end of words as in 'ha*t*' and 'ha*d*', and in the middle of words as in 'h*a*t' and 'h*o*t'.

When learners have been taught a group of sounds they can then learn to blend the sounds to read words made up from those sounds. They can then be taught more sounds and learn to blend those too.

The order in which the sounds are taught will vary depending on which scheme is used in your school, but it shouldn't be alphabetical order as that is not the best order to allow learners to start blending the sounds for reading.

Some sounds are represented by more than one letter such as *sh* in '*sh*ip', *ch* in '*ch*at.

The powerful reason for looking at alphabet letters as sounds is to give learners a tool to read words and they must be encouraged to do so at all times. It is important for learners to know the sounds. It is more important for them to use the sounds as a reading strategy.

Concept of rhyme – Learners should also be given the opportunity to develop the concept of rhyme. They should have plenty of opportunities to become familiar with rhymes through listening to, joining in with and reciting and performing rhymes. When learners experience singing, chanting and learning rhymes they gradually develop a script for building rhyming skills through imitation and experimenting.

The three elements of rhyme are:

- an awareness of rhyme
- the ability to recognise and identify rhyme
- the ability to generate rhyme.

Segmenting and blending – Learners should be given every opportunity to develop an appreciation of blending individual sounds to make words, e.g. *c-a-t*/'cat', *sh-o-p*/'shop' and *b-oa-t*/'boat', and segmenting words into sounds, e.g. 'cat'/*c-a-t*, 'shop'/*sh-o-p* and 'boat'/*b-oa-t*.

They should be given opportunities to build words with letters using their sense of analogy and to see the resemblance between certain words. They should be given opportunities to read new words by changing the initial sound (onset) and by using the rime from the original word. For example:

hat	best	hop	boat
bat	nest	top	coat
fat	pest	shop	moat
sat	rest	chop	float

At the early stages every day should include some phonic activity. This may be in the form of direct teaching, reading lists of regular words, writing regular words (or using magnetic letters to form words), phonic games and activities, and recapping/highlighting a phonic skill that arises from a text. You should take every opportunity to reinforce the learners' learning by asking about/commenting on phonic skills recently taught.

Learning objectives matching grid

The types of reading texts and the objectives covered in each unit are listed here by strand for easy reference. These same objectives are listed at the beginning of each unit in the unit-by-unit support section of this book.

Unit 1	Reading	Writing	Speaking and listening
Going places Texts: *The Big Red Bus* (simple recount with familiar settings) *Let's Go Shopping* (non-fiction text) *Simple map of bus route* (labels and captions) *Dan, Dan* (simple rhyme)	1R01 Hear, read and write initial letter sounds. 1R04 Use knowledge of sounds to read and write single-syllable words with short vowels. 1R06 Use phonic knowledge to read decodable words and to attempt to sound out some elements of unfamiliar words. 1R09 Know that in English, print is read from left to right and top to bottom. 1R10 Read a range of common words on sight. 1R12 Make links to own experiences. 1R14 Learn and recite simple poems. 1R16 Read aloud independently from simple books. 1R17 Pause at full stops when reading. 1R18 Identify sentences in a text. 1Rx1 Read labels, lists and captions to find information. 1Ri2 Talk about events in a story and make simple inferences about characters and events to show understanding. 1Rw2 Recognise story elements, e.g. beginning, middle and end 1Rv2 Know the parts of a book, e.g. title page, contents.	1W03 Know that a capital letter is used for 'I', for proper nouns and for the start of a sentence. 1W04 Use knowledge of sounds to write simple regular words, and to attempt other words including when writing simple sentences dictated by the teacher from memory. 1Wa2 Use relevant vocabulary. 1Wa3 Record answers to questions, e.g. as lists, charts. 1Wa6 Write simple information texts with labels, captions, lists, questions and instructions for a purpose. 1Wt1 Write a sequence of sentences retelling a familiar story or recounting an experience. 1Wp2 Compose and write a simple sentence with a capital letter and a full stop. 1Wp3 Write sentence-like structures which may be joined by 'and'. 1Ws3 Use rhyme and relate this to spelling patterns.	1SL1 Speak clearly and choose words carefully to express feelings and ideas when speaking of matters of immediate interest. 1SL2 Converse audibly with friends, teachers and other adults. 1SL4 Answer questions and explain further when asked. 1SL6 Take turns in speaking. 1SL7 Listen to others and respond appropriately. 1SL9 Engage in imaginative play, enacting simple characters or situations. 1SL10 Note that people speak in different ways for different purposes and meanings.

Unit 2	Reading	Writing	Speaking and listening
I can do Texts: *Max Can Do It!* (simple story with a familiar setting)	1R02 Know the name of, and most common sound associated with, every letter in the English alphabet. 1R03 Identify separate sounds (phonemes) within words, which may be represented by more than one letter, e.g. *th*, *ch*, *sh*. 1R04 Use knowledge of sounds to read and write single-syllable words with short vowels. 1R06 Use phonic knowledge to read decodable words and to attempt to sound out some elements of unfamiliar words. 1R07 Demonstrate an understanding that one spoken word corresponds with one written word. 1R08 Join in with reading familiar, simple stories and poems. 1R09 Know that in English, print is read from left to right and top to bottom. 1R10 Read a range of common words on sight. 1R12 Make links to own experiences. 1R13 Retell stories, with some appropriate use of story language. 1R16 Read aloud independently from simple books. 1R17 Pause at full stops when reading. 1Ri2 Talk about events in a story and make simple inferences about characters and events to show understanding.	1W03 Know that a capital letter is used for 'I', for proper nouns and for the start of a sentence. 1W06 Develop strategies to build vocabulary. 1Wt1 Write a sequence of sentences retelling a familiar story or recounting an experience. 1Wp2 Compose and write a simple sentence with a capital letter and a full stop. 1Wp3 Write sentence-like structures which may be joined by 'and'. 1Ws3 Use rhyme and relate this to spelling patterns. 1Ws4 Recognise common word endings, e.g. *–s*, *–ed* and *–ing*.	1SL3 Show some awareness of the listener through non-verbal communication. 1SL6 Take turns in speaking. 1SL7 Listen to others and respond appropriately. 1SL8 Listen carefully to questions and instructions. 1SL9 Engage in imaginative play, enacting simple characters or situations.

	1Rw1 Talk about significant aspects of a story's language, e.g. repetitive refrain, rhyme, patterned language. 1Rw2 Recognise story elements, e.g. beginning, middle and end. 1Rv2 Know the parts of a book, e.g. title page, contents.		
Unit 3	**Reading**	**Writing**	**Speaking and listening**
Let's find out Texts: *In the forest* *Animal Coats* *Cats* (non-fiction information texts) *Lion* (simple rhyme) *Foxes* (non-fiction, fact file) *Five Little Ducks* (traditional rhyme)	1R03 Identify separate sounds (phonemes) within words, which may be represented by more than one letter, e.g. *th*, *ch*, *sh*. 1R06 Use phonic knowledge to read decodable words and to attempt to sound out some elements of unfamiliar words. 1R08 Join in with reading familiar, simple stories and poems. 1R09 Know that in English, print is read from left to right and top to bottom. 1R10 Read a range of common words on sight. 1R11 Enjoy reading and listening to a range of books, drawing on background information and vocabulary provided. 1R16 Read aloud independently from simple books. 1Rx1 Read labels, lists and captions to find information. 1Rv1 Show awareness that texts for different purposes look different, e.g. use of photographs, diagrams.	1W03 Know that a capital letter is used for 'I', for proper nouns and for the start of a sentence. 1W04 Use knowledge of sounds to write simple regular words, and to attempt other words, including when writing simple sentences dictated by the teacher from memory. 1Wa2 Use relevant vocabulary. 1Wa3 Record answers to questions, e.g. as lists, charts. 1Wa5 Write for a purpose using some basic features of text type. 1Wt1 Write a sequence of sentences retelling a familiar story or recounting an experience. 1Wp2 Compose and write a simple sentence with a capital letter and a full stop.	1SL1 Speak clearly and choose words carefully to express feelings and ideas when speaking of matters of immediate interest. 1SL2 Converse audibly with friends, teachers and other adults. 1SL3 Show some awareness of the listener through non-verbal communication. 1SL4 Answer questions and explain further when asked. 1SL6 Take turns in speaking. 1SL7 Listen to others and respond appropriately.

	1Rv2 Know the parts of a book, e.g. title page, contents.	1Ws4 Recognise common word endings, e.g. –s, –ed and –ing.	
Unit 4	**Reading**	**Writing**	**Speaking and listening**
The moon Texts: *Bot on the Moon* (fantasy story) *Mister Moon* (poetry)	1R05 Blend to read, and segment to spell words with final and initial adjacent consonants, e.g. *b-l, n-d.* 1R06 Use phonic knowledge to read decodable words and to attempt to sound out some elements of unfamiliar words. 1R08 Join in with reading familiar, simple stories and poems. 1R09 Know that in English, print is read from left to right and top to bottom. 1R10 Read a range of common words on sight. 1R12 Make links to own experiences. 1R13 Retell stories, with some appropriate use of story language. 1R16 Read aloud independently from simple books. 1R17 Pause at full stops when reading. 1R18 Identify sentences in a text. 1Ri2 Talk about events in a story and make simple inferences about characters and events to show understanding. 1Rw2 Recognise story elements, e.g. beginning, middle and end.	1Wa2 Use relevant vocabulary. 1Wt1 Write a sequence of sentences retelling a familiar story or recounting an experience. 1Wa3 Record answers to questions, e.g. as lists, charts. 1Wt1 Write a sequence of sentences retelling a familiar story or recounting an experience. 1Wp1 Mark some sentence endings with a full stop. 1Wa5 Write for a purpose using some basic features of text type. 1Wa1 Write simple storybooks with sentences to caption pictures. 1Ws3 Use rhyme and relate this to spelling patterns.	1SL3 Show some awareness of the listener through non-verbal communication 1SL6 Take turns in speaking 1SL7 Listen to others and respond appropriately 1SL4 Answer questions and explain further when asked

Unit 5	Reading	Writing	Speaking and listening
Funny Fish Texts: *Funny Fish* (story with patterned and predictable language.) *A Fine Feathered Fish* (nonsense poem) *Nut Tree* (Teacher's Guide only) (rhyming poem)	1R02 Know the name of, and most common sound associated with, every letter in the English alphabet. 1R05 Blend to read, and segment to spell, words with final and initial adjacent consonants, e.g. *b-l, n-d.* 1R06 Use phonic knowledge to read decodable words and to attempt to sound out some elements of unfamiliar words. 1R10 Read a range of common words on sight. 1R14 Learn and recite simple poems. 1R15 Join in and extend rhymes and refrains, playing with language patterns. 1R16 Read aloud independently from simple books. 1Ri2 Talk about events in a story and make simple inferences about characters and events to show understanding. 1Rw2 Recognise story elements, e.g. beginning, middle and end. 1Rv2 Know the parts of a book, e.g. title page, contents.	1W03 Know that a capital letter is used for 'I', for proper nouns and for the start of a sentence. 1Wa2 Use relevant vocabulary. 1Wa3 Record answers to questions, e.g. as lists, charts. 1Wt1 Write a sequence of sentences retelling a familiar story or recounting an experience. 1Wp2 Compose and write a simple sentence with a capital letter and a full stop. 1Ws1 Begin to learn common spellings of long vowel phonemes, e.g. *ee, ai, oo.* 1Ws2 Spell familiar common words accurately, drawing on sight vocabulary. 1Ws3 Use rhyme and relate this to spelling patterns. 1Ws4 Recognise common word endings, e.g. *–s, –ed* and *–ing.*	1SL1 Speak clearly and choose words carefully to express feelings and ideas when speaking of matters of immediate interest. 1SL2 Converse audibly with friends, teachers and other adults. 1SL3 Show some awareness of the listener through non-verbal communication. 1SL6 Take turns in speaking. 1SL7 Listen to others and respond appropriately. 1SL8 Listen carefully to questions and instructions.

Unit 6	Reading	Writing	Speaking and listening
Food Texts: *Pie diagram* (non-fiction, labels and headings) *Fish and seafood* *Fruit and vegetables* *Dairy and eggs* *Bread and cereals* *Sugar and fats* (non-fiction texts)	1R05 Blend to read, and segment to spell, words with final and initial adjacent consonants, e.g. *b-l, n-d.* 1R06 Use phonic knowledge to read decodable words and to attempt to sound out some elements of unfamiliar words. 1R10 Read a range of common words on sight. 1R11 Enjoy reading and listening to a range of books, drawing on background information and vocabulary provided. 1R12 Make links to own experiences. 1R16 Read aloud independently from simple books. 1R18 Identify sentences in a text. 1Rx1 Read labels, lists and captions to find information.	1W03 Know that a capital letter is used for 'I', for proper nouns and for the start of a sentence. 1W06 Develop strategies to build vocabulary. 1Wa1 Write simple storybooks with sentences to caption pictures. 1Wa2 Use relevant vocabulary. 1Wa4 Begin to use some formulaic language, e.g. 'Once upon a time'. 1Wa6 Write simple information texts with labels, captions, lists, questions and instructions for a purpose. 1Wt1 Write a sequence of sentences retelling a familiar story or recounting an experience. 1Wp2 Compose and write a simple sentence with a capital letter and a full stop. 1Ws2 Spell familiar common words accurately, drawing on sight vocabulary. 1Ws3 Use rhyme and relate this to spelling patterns.	1SL2 Converse audibly with friends, teachers and other adults. 1SL4 Answer questions and explain further when asked. 1SL5 Speak confidently to a group to share an experience. 1SL6 Take turns in speaking. 1SL7 Listen to others and respond appropriately.

Unit 7	Reading	Writing	Speaking and listening
Traditional stories Texts: *The Small Bun* (traditional story) *Recipe* (instructions)	1R06 Use phonic knowledge to read decodable words and to attempt to sound out some elements of unfamiliar words. 1R08 Join in with reading familiar, simple stories and poems. 1R10 Read a range of common words on sight. 1R13 Retell stories, with some appropriate use of story language. 1R16 Read aloud independently from simple books. 1R17 Pause at full stops when reading. 1Ri1 Anticipate what happens next in a story. 1Ri2 Talk about events in a story and make simple inferences about characters and events to show understanding.	1Wa1 Write simple storybooks with sentences to caption pictures. 1Wa2 Use relevant vocabulary. 1Wt1 Write a sequence of sentences retelling a familiar story or recounting an experience. 1Wp2 Compose and write a simple sentence with a capital letter and a full stop. 1Ws1 Begin to learn common spellings of long vowel phonemes, e.g. *ee*, *ai*, *oo*. 1Ws2 Spell familiar common words accurately, drawing on sight vocabulary. 1Ws3 Use rhyme and relate this to spelling patterns.	1SL4 Answer questions and explain further when asked. 1SL5 Speak confidently to a group to share an experience. 1SL6 Take turns in speaking. 1SL7 Listen to others and respond appropriately. 1SL8 Listen carefully to questions and instructions.

Unit 8	Reading	Writing	Speaking and listening
Feelings Texts: *The Lonely Penguin* (story with predictable structure and patterned language) *Penguins* (non-fiction fact file)	1R06 Use phonic knowledge to read decodable words and to attempt to sound out some elements of unfamiliar words. 1R08 Join in with reading familiar, simple stories and poems. 1R10 Read a range of common words on sight. 1R13 Retell stories, with some appropriate use of story language. 1R16 Read aloud independently from simple books. 1Ri1 Anticipate what happens next in a story. 1Ri2 Talk about events in a story and make simple inferences about characters and events to show understanding.	1Wa2 Use relevant vocabulary. 1Wa4 Begin to use some formulaic language, e.g. 'Once upon a time'. 1Wt1 Write a sequence of sentences retelling a familiar story or recounting an experience. 1Wp2 Compose and write a simple sentence with a capital letter and a full stop 1Ws1 Begin to learn common spellings of long vowel phonemes, e.g. *ee*, *ai*, *oo*. 1Ws2 Spell familiar common words accurately, drawing on sight vocabulary. 1Ws3 Use rhyme and relate this to spelling patterns. 1Ws4 Recognise common word endings, e.g. *–s*, *–ed* and *–ing*.	1SL1 Speak clearly and choose words carefully to express feelings and ideas when speaking of matters of immediate interest. 1SL2 Converse audibly with friends, teachers and other adults. 1SL6 Take turns in speaking. 1SL7 Listen to others and respond appropriately. 1SL4 Answer questions and explain further when asked.

18

Unit 9	Reading	Writing	Speaking and listening
Catching the Moon Texts: *Catching the Moon* (story with a familiar setting)	1R03 Identify separate sounds (phonemes) within words, which may be represented by more than one letter, e.g. *th*, *ch*, *sh*. 1R06 Use phonic knowledge to read decodable words and to attempt to sound out some elements of unfamiliar words. 1R10 Read a range of common words on sight. 1R11 Enjoy reading and listening to a range of books, drawing on background information and vocabulary provided. 1R12 Make links to own experiences. 1R13 Retell stories, with some appropriate use of story language. 1R16 Read aloud independently from simple books. 1R17 Pause at full stops when reading. 1Ri2 Talk about events in a story and make simple inferences about characters and events to show understanding. 1Rw2 Recognise story elements, e.g. beginning, middle and end.	1W03 Know that a capital letter is used for 'I', for proper nouns and for the start of a sentence. 1W04 Use knowledge of sounds to write simple regular words, and to attempt other words including when writing simple sentences dictated by the teacher from memory. 1W05 Read own writing aloud and talk about it. 1Wa2 Use relevant vocabulary. 1Wa3 Record answers to questions, e.g. as lists, charts. 1Wa6 Write simple information texts with labels, captions, lists, questions and instructions for a purpose. 1Wp2 Compose and write a simple sentence with a capital letter and a full stop. 1Ws3 Use rhyme and relate this to spelling patterns.	1SL3 Show some awareness of the listener through non-verbal communication. 1SL4 Answer questions and explain further when asked. 1SL6 Take turns in speaking. 1SL7 Listen to others and respond appropriately. 1SL9 Engage in imaginative play, enacting simple characters or situations. 1SL10 Note that people speak in different ways for different purposes and meanings.

Note that handwriting is not taught explicitly in this course although objectives 'W01 Develop a comfortable and efficient pencil grip', and 'W02 Form letters correctly', are implicitly covered in the activities and supporting notes in the Teacher's Guide. We recommend that teachers choose a structured and suitable course for teaching handwriting skills at Stage 1 level. The *Collins Treasure House* series is a useful resource for this, progressing from the introduction of fine motor skills, through pre-cursive and cursive styles at the early stages, then to different handwriting styles, calligraphy and links to computer fonts at higher levels

Unit 1 Going places

Unit overview

As learners work through this unit, they will read a story aloud and then retell and talk about the events in the story. *The Big Red Bus* is a simple story with familiar settings. Extracts introduce a non-fiction report. Learners will also read and memorise a simple rhyme. They will learn about the layout of lists and signs before writing their own.

The unit could be part of a study of different types of transport and/or a study of the local area.

Learners will have opportunities to develop hearing and identifying phonemes in words, and to segment and blend phonemes to spell and read words in isolation and embedded in text.

They will have opportunities to read high frequency words and other familiar words.

Reading	Writing	Speaking and listening
1R01 Hear, read and write initial letter sounds.	1W03 Know that a capital letter is used for I, for proper nouns and for the start of a sentence.	1SL1 Speak clearly and choose words carefully to express feelings and ideas when speaking of matters of immediate interest.
1R04 Use knowledge of sounds to read and write single syllable words with short vowels.	1W04 Use knowledge of sounds to write simple regular words, and to attempt other words including when writing simple sentences dictated by the teacher from memory.	1SL2 Converse audibly with friends, teachers and other adults.
1R06 Use phonic knowledge to read decodable words and to attempt to sound out some elements of unfamiliar words.		
1R09 Know that in English, print is read from left to right and top to bottom.		1SL4 Answer questions and explain further when asked.
1R10 Read a range of common words on sight.	1Wa2 Use relevant vocabulary.	
	1Wa3 Record answers to questions, e.g. as lists, charts.	1SL6 Take turns in speaking.
1R12 Make links to own experiences.		
1R14 Learn and recite simple poems.	1Wa6 Write simple information texts with labels, captions, lists, questions and instructions for a purpose.	1SL7 Listen to others and respond appropriately.
1R16 Read aloud independently from simple books.		1SL9 Engage in imaginative play, enacting simple characters or situations.
1R17 Pause at full stops when reading.	1Wt1 Write a sequence of sentences retelling a familiar story or recounting an experience.	
1R18 Identify sentences in a text.		
1Rx1 Read labels, lists and captions to find information.	1Wp2 Compose and write a simple sentence with a capital letter and a full stop.	1SL10 Note that people speak in different ways for different purposes and meanings.
1Ri2 Talk about events in a story and make simple inferences about characters and events to show understanding.		
	1Wp3 Write sentence-like structures which may be joined by 'and'.	
1Rw2 Recognise story elements, e.g. beginning, middle and end.		
1Rv2 Know the parts of a book, e.g. title page, contents.	1Ws3 Use rhyme and relate this to spelling patterns.	

Related resources

- Audio file: *The Big Red Bus*
- Slideshow 1: Going places
- Image 1: *The Big Red Bus* front cover
- PCMs 1–8: Phonics
- PCM 9: End of unit assessment

Introducing the unit

The unit could be introduced by showing learners some pictures of different types of transport, for example, bicycles, boats, cars, buses, aeroplanes, trains, vans and trucks, leading to a discussion on their similarities and differences. You can then move on to discuss the different means of transport that learners might use, and when they might use each type.

If there is time, put learners in pairs or small groups. Give each learner a different type of transport (a picture of a vehicle or a card with the name of a vehicle on it). Learners should not show each other their cards. Ask them to take turns to describe the type of transport to each other; their partner or group tries to guess what is being described

Week 1

Student's Book pages 1–6

Workbook pages 1–3

The focus this week is on familiarising learners with story books and how they work. They will learn to read from left to right and to apply a range of strategies for decoding unfamiliar words. They will also join in with reading and complete a range of activities that demonstrate their understanding of what they have read.

Workbook page 1

Vocabulary: transport words

In this activity learners match the words with the pictures.

Remind learners to use phonic clues to work out words. Only two words begin with the same letter so initial sounds should help for most words. 'Boat' and 'bus' both start with *b* so what should they do to work out what sound comes next? Most learners will recognise 'bus' or be able to sound it out. If not, it is important to help them to use strategies, for example, to look for other clues. The word 'bus' ends with *s* and 'boat' ends with *t*. Always encourage learners to look for ways of working out what a word says.

Student's Book page 1

Listening and speaking

Give learners the opportunity to try to read the instructions in pairs or on their own before inviting one learner to read them aloud. Model correct reading and ensure that learners understand what is being asked of them before giving them time to do the activity.

Draw the class together for a discussion.

Extension: Choose one or more of the topics discussed, for example, how learners travel to school. Ask learners to collect data from a suitable number of their peers (at least eight) to answer the question. They can use a table or tallies to do this. Once they have collected the data, ask them to use it to draw a simple pictograph or block graph to display their findings. Make sure they label the graph correctly and that they give it a heading to make its meaning clear. (See the mathematics framework for more information on this topic if necessary.)

Vocabulary: transport words

1 Check that learners can read the words below the pictures before moving on to the questions in activity 2.

2 Give learners the opportunity to work in pairs to read the questions. Then draw them together to ensure understanding before they do the activity. Refer back to pictures of different types of transport to reinforce learning.

Remind learners to use the picture clues to help them to read the third question by linking it to the labelled picture of a bicycle in activity 1.

Highlight the question words 'What' and 'How many'. Invite learners to give examples of questions beginning with 'What' and 'How many'. Then ask them to answer each other's questions. For example:

- What is your name?
- What colour is your hair?
- How many feet do you have?
- How many girls are in the class?

3 Give learners some time to draw and label their pictures. Alternatively, they can cut out pictures from newspapers or magazines and use those instead of drawing.

Student's Book page 2

Reading and writing

Display the picture of the cover of *The Big Red Bus* (as on page 2 of the Student's Book) and spend some time ensuring that learners know the terms 'title' and 'illustrator'. Use other books in the classroom to highlight features such as the title, the author's name and the illustrator's name. (Some books are written and illustrated by the same person.)

Give learners the opportunity to try to read the section by themselves or in pairs before drawing them together to ensure that they can read and understand the questions.

Highlight 'Who' and 'What' questions. Invite learners to give examples of 'Who' and 'What' questions. For example:

- Who lives in your house?
- Who is going to the park to play?
- What is your friend's name?
- What school do you go to?

Support/Extension: Some learners may give answers orally whilst others may write answers.

Answers
1 The Big Red Bus   **2** It is big and red.
3 Alison Hawes   **4** a big red bus

Workbook page 2

Reading and writing

In this activity learners add details to a picture to complete a scene.

Before asking learners to do the activity, discuss where the bus might be going and write some suggestions on the whiteboard. Once learners have completed the task, discuss what else could be added to the picture and/or how the scene might look in their community.

Extension: Ask learners to draw up a list or table of similarities and differences between the scene shown and what they would see at a bus stop in their own community.

Student's Book pages 2–5

Reading and listening

1 Before learners do the activity, it would be worth recapping good reading practices with them. Then read the story aloud to the class or play the audio file whilst they follow and listen.

Remind learners where they should start reading. Ask them to point to the first word and then run their finger along the print in the direction that they should read. Remind them that every word on the page has a spoken word correspondence when they read.

Tell learners that when they are following a text while someone else is reading, they should be reading along 'in their head'. They may need to be prompted occasionally, so ask questions, for example: 'Put your finger on the last word that I read. What is the next word?'

Remember that questioning should be done in such a way that it does not focus attention on learners who need support. Some learners could become anxious and this does not help with their reading.

Tell learners you are going to read the story again. This time, while they listen, they have to think about two things. Refer to the text and ask learners to read the questions and say what they have to listen for. Then ask them to follow as they listen to the audio file or you reading the story again.

2 Spend as much time as necessary on this section to ensure correct decoding of the text and to encourage reading with fluency. Encourage learners to use a variety of strategies, for example, phonic skills, picture and context clues, reading on and rereading, to decipher any unknown word.

Support: Some learners may need teacher support, individually or as part of a small group, to use these strategies when decoding the text.

Answers
1 Nut Hill; Grandad

Student's Book page 6

Reading and writing

Before turning to the activities on page 6 of the Student's Book and page 3 of the Workbook, ensure that learners understand the text by asking questions. For example:

- Where did the children sit on the bus?
- Who was waiting at the bus stop?
- Why do you think the children grab on to the rail?

Spend some time developing the concepts of 'true' and 'false' with learners before attempting the activities.

The following activity can be used to develop the concepts of 'true' and 'false'. Make a number of statements and ask learners to say whether each one is true or not. Point out that 'true' means 'correct', and 'false' means 'not correct'. For example:

- Birds can fly.
- Trees have leaves.
- The grass is red.
- A car has wheels.
- A frog can fly.
- 4 + 4 = 7

Examples should relate to the learners' own environment.

Invite learners to make statements; the rest of the class answer 'true' or 'false'.

Extension: Ask learners to write two true and two false statements on cards. This activity could be linked to a topic they are learning about, such as transport, birds or farming, or to mathematics. They can then play a game in small groups. Each learner turns over a card and the person to their left has to say whether it is true or false.

Answers
1 The bus is going to Nut Hill.
2 The bus went past the pond.
4 You press the bell to get off.

Workbook page 3

Reading and writing

This section assesses learners' decoding of a familiar text and understanding of the story. Learners have to match the beginning of sentences with their endings.

Highlight the word 'I' in the story on pages 10 and 12. Explain the use of a capital letter for 'I'. Note that here 'I' is at the beginning of a sentence, but 'I' always has a capital letter wherever it appears as a word. Write some simple sentences on the whiteboard to show this. For example:

- When I am tired, I go to bed.
- I like dhal.
- In the morning I wash my face.

Answers
1 We sit at the back of the bus.; We grab on to the rail.; The bus is fast.; I press the bell to get off.

Weekly review

Use this rubric to assess learners' progress as they worked through the activities this week.

Level	Reading
■	This group can read the story with assistance and recognise some sight words but do not consistently apply strategies for decoding unfamiliar words.
●	This group can read the story and recognise sight words but do not consistently apply strategies for decoding unfamiliar words.
▲	This group can read the story confidently on their own and use a range of strategies to decode words they do not know.

Week 2

Student's Book pages 6–7

Workbook pages 4–6

The focus of this week's work is retelling the story, identifying and using words from the story, and phonic skills.

Whilst phonic skills should be part of the daily programme at this stage, the activities in this week's work are designed to give further practice in reading and writing consonant-vowel-consonant (CVC) words and in developing the concept of rhyme. Learners need to use knowledge of sounds to read and write CVC words. For this reason, these words are presented in lists rather than in a context to make sure learners decode them rather than use contextual cues to make a sensible guess what the word is.

Student's Book page 6

Sounds and spelling

1 Recap understanding of initial sounds in words by asking learners to say, show and/or write the initial sound of spoken words.

2 Ensure understanding of the concept of writing words in lists. For example, write four words – 'red', 'yellow', 'green' and 'blue' – in a list on the whiteboard. Ask learners what they notice about the words and how they are written. (They are all colours and they are written one below the other.) Explain that a list is a number of connected items or names written consecutively, and usually one below the other.

3 Learners look at the pictures and practise writing CVC words.

Support: Magnetic letters could be used for this activity. These allow learners to focus on choosing the correct letters to spell words without having to think about how to form the letters.

Extension: This is an ideal opportunity to focus on broad writing skills and letter formation. Ask learners to write words using different styles, sizes of letters and colours to decorate them and allude to their meaning. For example, the word 'red' could be written in red pencil, or the word 'big' could be written in letters that are much bigger than the others. Allow for creative use of fonts and for learners to play with computer printing if this is available.

Answers

2

cap	big	map
cot	but	mix
can	bat	man

3 bus; bag; bin; bed

Student's Book page 7

Reading and speaking

Before asking learners to retell the story, ask them to reread it, individually or in pairs.

A good follow-up to the retelling of the story would be to ask questions about the events in the story. For example:

- What happened at the beginning in the story?
- Where was the bus going to?
- What did the children do first when they got on the bus?
- What did they do next?
- Why do you think they had to grab on to the rail?
- What did they do before they got off the bus?
- What did the little girl do after she got off the bus?
- The little girl was going to meet her grandfather. Where do you think the other people were going?

Support: Work to support individuals or small groups as needed.

Writing

1–2 In this section learners are asked to read sentences from the story and to choose and write the sentence that comes at the beginning of the story and the sentence that comes at the end of the story. They then write the sentences in the correct order.

Answers
1 We get on the bus.
2 We get on the bus. We sit at the back of the bus. We pass the duck pond. Grandad is at the bus stop.

Workbook page 4

Reading and writing

In this section learners are asked to use words from the story; the words are not embedded in the text.

24

1 Learners choose and write words that describe the bus.

2 Learners label pictures.

3 Learners complete and copy sentences.

Remind learners to use clues to work out any unknown words.

Answers
1 red, big
2 top left: clock; top right: duck pond; bottom left: bell; bottom right: bus stop
3 red; stop

Workbook page 5

Sounds and spelling

This activity requires close reading by learners. There is only one letter that is different in each pair of words: the initial consonant, the vowel or the final consonant.

Before turning to page 5, learners should practise reading pairs of words where only one letter is different, for example: 'tin' – 'tan', 'cot' – 'cat', 'lid' – 'did', 'top' – 'hop', 'rug' – 'rub' and 'pet' – 'pen'.

After learners have read a pair of words, ask them which sound (beginning, middle or end) is different in each pair.

PCMs 1–6 give further practice in reading and writing CVC words. They should be used, now or later, for all or some learners as needed.

PCMs 1–3 have a particular focus on reading pairs of words where only one letter is different.

PCMs 4–5 focus on writing CVC words.

PCM 6 focuses on reading CVC words in context.

Ask learners to turn to page 5 of the Workbook and do the activity.

Answers
bin; bag; zip; hat; jug; cat

Workbook page 6

Reading and writing

1 This activity provides further work on reading CVC words. Once learners have read them, they write them in lists that rhyme.

2 Work with learners to create lists of rhyming words. If necessary, help them with one or two words.

3 This simple rhyme is based on a traditional Irish nursery rhyme. The complete rhyme is:

| Dan, Dan, the funny old man, |
| Washed his face in the frying pan, |
| Combed his hair with the leg of the chair, |
| Dan, Dan, the funny old man. |

Read it with learners and have them work out the missing word. Once they have done that, ask them to read and memorise the rhyme so they can recite it. Most learners should manage the four-line complete version.

PCMs 7–8 give further practice in CVC words that rhyme. Use these now or later as needed.

Support: Use PCMs 7–8 to reinforce rhyming words and the spelling of CVC words with learners who are struggling. You may also like to play some word games involving rhyming words. For example:

1 Listen for the rhyme

Stick or draw a picture on the whiteboard. Then say a list of words and ask learners to raise their hand when they hear a word that rhymes with the picture.

- Example 1: 'chair'
  Suggested words: 'bear', 'cat', 'garden', 'hair', 'stair', 'tree', 'wear', 'pear', 'stone', 'fair', 'bush', 'bucket', 'where'
- Example 2: 'zip'.
  Suggested words: 'drip', 'run', 'ship', 'lip', 'pie', 'hip', 'ten', 'pip', 'chip', 'go', 'box', 'tip', 'dip', 'lid'.

2 Ask for the rhyming words

Prepare strips with overlapping pairs of rhyming words. For this activity to work, you need pairs of words. Each word must appear in the first sentence of one card and the question of another. For example:

| I have jet. Who has pet? |
| I have pet. Who has met? |
| I have met. Who has net? |
| I have net. Who has set? |
| I have set. Who has jet? |

Give each learner a strip and decide who will start. The first person reads their strip and the person with the correct word then reads theirs.

Extension: Quicker learners can spend some time making up silly rhymes based on the words they have learnt and others they know. They can either do this orally or write (and illustrate) them. For example:

- A fat cat with a hat …
- A fat cat with a hat sat on a mat.
- A hen with a pen …
- A hen with a pen counted to ten.

There is a wide range of CVC word rhyming and spelling activities on the internet.

Dictation: At this level, learners need to develop their writing skills at the same time as they are learning to use sounds to write simple words. Use simple phrases and sentences as class dictation on a regular basis to help develop these skills. To encourage listening and thinking skills, instruct learners first to listen carefully to the phrases and/or sentences with their pencils down. Initially, a phrase/sentence may need to be repeated to help learners to memorise it before they are asked to write it down. Use one or two sentences per day.

For example:

- A red bus.
- A hot pot.
- Ten men.
- A fat hen.
- A dog sat on a mat.
- Ted is in the red bed.
- The man is in a big van.
- The fox sat on the box.
- Jez had a cup and a mug.
- Sam has a pen and a zip.

Answers

2

jug	pan	net
tug	fan	get
hug	man	pet
bug	tan	set
rug	can	met

3 pan

Weekly review

Use this rubric to assess learners' progress as they worked through the activities this week.

Level	Reading	Writing
■	This group can read consonant-vowel-consonant words. Further practice is needed to improve accuracy and speed.	This group can write most consonant-vowel-consonant words accurately. They cope well with medial *a*, *o*, and *e* but need more practice with medial *u* and medial *i*.
●	This group can read consonant-vowel-consonant words with accuracy.	This group can write consonant-vowel-consonant words accurately to dictation and are making good progress in their own writing.
▲	This group can read consonant-vowel-consonant words with speed and accuracy.	This group can write consonant-vowel-consonant words accurately to dictation and in their own writing.

Week 3

Student's Book pages 8–10

Workbook pages 7–9

The focus of this week's work is non-fiction books. It is important to give learners

opportunities to explore and investigate a selection of books.

Discuss what makes non-fiction books (factual books or information books) different from fiction books (stories), for example: the layout, photographs, diagrams, signs and captions. Learners will have the opportunity to record information in lists and to write signs and captions.

In addition to the work on books and texts, the Workbook contains focused activities on the alphabet and on the vowels in particular. The following rhymes/songs will help learners to learn alphabetical order and the sound that each letter has:

The A [name] says ah, [sound]
The A says ah,
Every letter makes a sound,
The A says ah.

The B says buh,
The B says buh,
Every letter makes a sound,
The B says buh.

(and so on through the alphabet)

A B C D E F G [gee]
H I J K L M N O P [pee]
Q R S T U and V [vee]
W X Y and Z [zee]
Now I know my ABC,
Come along and sing with me.

Here is a mnemonic to help learners remember the vowels:

angry   elephants   in   orange   underwear

a   **e**   **i**   **o**   **u**

Extension: Learners can make up and illustrate a mnemonic of their own.

Student's Book page 8

Reading and speaking

Before learners do the activities in this section, take opportunities to find and discuss signs in the environment – the classroom, school and/or their local environment – or display a picture of signs.

You could take learners on a 'sign walk' to find signs in and around the school. Use a school camera to take photographs of the signs and display them in the classroom later.

Signs that there may be around the school include: Office; Dining hall; Boys' toilets; Girls' toilets; School entrance; Parking for staff; All visitors must report to the school office.

Ask learners to do activities 1 and 2.

Writing

Discuss how signs are written and why they are written in a certain way. For example, visual impact is important; capital letters are often used; signs need to be bold and uncluttered. Ask learners to suggest reasons for this.

Discuss with learners the difference between a list and continuous text. Ask them when they last wrote lists (they did this when they wrote rhyming words) and show them other lists, for example: shopping lists, telephone numbers and lists of names. Model writing a list.

Ask learners to do activities 1 and 2.

Role play

Encourage learners to think about how they might greet each other casually in the playground. Then talk about how they might greet other people, for example: teachers, adults, their elders and strangers in shops. Move on to a discussion about shopping in general and how you talk to people who are serving you in various places. Focus on politeness and the need to express or ask for what you want.

Spend some time talking about what a shopkeeper might ask or talk about. For example, the person in a shoe shop might ask about the type of shoe, size and colour the customer wants to look at. They may suggest different shoes or ask the customer if the shoes fit or if they are comfortable. The person shopping for shoes might ask/talk about the price, different colours, different sizes and whether the shoes are too small, too big or too tight.

Help learners to develop their conversations. Invite pairs to perform their role play for the rest of the class.

Student's Book page 9

Reading and writing

1 Before learners do this activity, show them examples of captions, ensuring that they understand that a caption is a short piece of text.

2 Before learners do this activity, ensure that they can identify the pictures.

Answers
1 This is the book shop.; This is the newsagents'.; This is the shoe shop.
2 pen; zip; pot; hat; bat; mug; mop; bed

Student's Book page 10

Reading
Activities 1–4

Before learners attempt activities 1–4, spend some time looking at book covers. Discuss types of books (fiction and non-fiction), authors and illustrators.

Images of covers of non-fiction books could be used here. (See **Related resources**.)

Answers
2 The story book is *Best Bird*.; She wrote *In the Forest*.; You can find out about cats in *Pet Cat, Big Cat*.; Claire Llewellyn wrote *Animal Coats*

Workbook pages 7–8
Sounds and spelling
Before attempting the activities in this section, learners could repeat the songs and rhymes they have learned to revise the alphabet and vowels. (See page 9.)

Answers
1 There are 26 letters in the alphabet.; There are five vowels in the alphabet.; a, e, i, o, u.
2 The missing letters are: d, g, j, l, m, o, p, r, s, v, x, y.

Workbook page 9
Sounds and spelling
This section assesses learners' understanding of vowels. Check the following:

- Can learners hear and identify vowel sounds in the middle of words?
- Can learners write the letters that represent the sounds?

Answers
bag; pot; lid; jug; net; hat; log; zip; sun; ten

Student's Book page 10
Reading
Activities 5–6

If necessary, allow learners to read *The Big Red Bus* again before they discuss why they liked or did not like the book.

Encourage learners to relate their own experience of travelling on a bus. Do they like travelling on buses? Why/why not?

Weekly review

Use this rubric to assess learners' progress as they worked through the activities this week.

Level	Reading	Listening and speaking
■	This group have some understanding of the difference between a fiction book and a non-fiction book. They can read lists, signs and captions in the context of a book with support.	This group engage in imaginative play, and with support can express themselves in the roles of different characters.
●	This group understand the difference between a fiction book and a non-fiction book. They can read lists, signs and captions in the context of a book with minimal support.	This group engage in imaginative play. They take on the roles of characters.
▲	This group understand the difference between a fiction book and a non-fiction book. They can read lists, signs and captions in the context of a book.	This group engage in imaginative play. They use different voices when they take on the roles of characters.

End of unit assessment
Use PCM 9 to assess whether learners can read and follow instructions and whether they can read sentences and sequence them to retell a familiar story. Observe learners as they work and note who can (or cannot) read and understand the instructions.

Check learners' completed work to make sure the sequence is correct. If this is not possible, ask learners to exchange their sentences with a partner and check and correct each other's work.

Self assessment
You will find a self-assessment chart on page 60 of the Workbook. Use this as you complete each unit, asking learners to tick the column that best applies to them. You can look at these to gain a sense of which learners feel they need more help and which are confident with their achievements.

Unit 2 I can do

Unit overview

As learners work through this unit, they will read a story aloud and then retell and talk about the events in the story. They will make simple inferences about characters and events to show understanding. *Max Can Do It!* is a simple story with a familiar setting.

The unit could be part of personal, social and emotional development – looking at making relationships, self-confidence and self-esteem.

Learners will begin to appreciate different aspects of a story's language, for example, direct speech. They will have the opportunity to read and write consonant-vowel-consonant (CVC) words, to read and write words where two letters represent one sound, and to use rhyme and relate it to spelling patterns. They will also have the opportunity to read and spell high frequency words and other familiar words.

Reading	Writing	Speaking and listening
1R02 Know the name of and most common sound associated with every letter in the English alphabet. 1R03 Identify separate sounds (phonemes) within words, which may be represented by more than one letter, e.g. *th*, *ch*, *sh*. 1R04 Use knowledge of sounds to read and write single syllable words with short vowels. 1R06 Use phonic knowledge to read decodable words and to attempt to sound out some elements of unfamiliar words. 1R07 Demonstrate an understanding that one spoken word corresponds with one written word. 1R08 Join in with reading familiar, simple stories and poems. 1R09 Know that in English, print is read from left to right and top to bottom. 1R10 Read a range of common words on sight. 1R12 Make links to own experiences. 1R13 Retell stories, with some appropriate use of story language. 1R16 Read aloud independently from simple books 1R17 Pause at full stops when reading. 1Ri2 Talk about events in a story and make simple inferences about characters and events to show understanding. 1Rw1 Talk about significant aspects of a story's language, e.g. repetitive refrain, rhyme, patterned language. 1Rw2 Recognise story elements, e.g. beginning, middle and end. 1Rv2 Know the parts of a book, e.g. title page, contents.	1W03 Know that a capital letter is used for 'I', for proper nouns and for the start of a sentence. 1W06 Develop strategies to build vocabulary. 1Wt1 Write a sequence of sentences retelling a familiar story or recounting an experience. 1Wp2 Compose and write a simple sentence with a capital letter and a full stop. 1Wp3 Write sentence-like structures which may be joined by 'and'. 1Ws3 Use rhyme and relate this to spelling patterns. 1Ws4 Recognise common word endings, e.g. *–s*, *–ed* and *–ing*.	1SL3 Show some awareness of the listener through non-verbal communication. 1SL6 Take turns in speaking. 1SL7 Listen to others and respond appropriately. 1SL8 Listen carefully to questions and instructions. 1SL9 Engage in imaginative play, enacting simple characters or situations.

Related resources:

- Audio file: *Max Can Do It!*
- Slideshow 2: I can do
- PCM 10: Words ending in *–ing*
- PCM 11: Phonics *– sh*
- PCMs 12–13 Phonics: *sh, ch, th, wh*
- PCM 14 End of unit assessment

Introducing the unit

The unit could be introduced by having a discussion with learners about what they can do and what they would like to be able to do. They could also have a discussion about feelings and how they feel when they cannot do things they would like to do, but that others can do. For example, some learners cannot tie their own shoelaces; others cannot swim, and so on.

Week 1

Student's Book pages 11–15

Workbook pages 10–12

Student's Book pages 11–14

Listening and speaking

Give learners the opportunity to try to read the instructions in pairs and then on their own before inviting a learner to read them aloud. Model correct reading and ensure that learners understand what is being asked of them before setting them to do the activity.

Draw the class together for a discussion. Check if there is something many learners would like to be able to do and that could be arranged at school, for example, some learners might like to learn to knit or play basketball.

Reading and writing

Have a discussion about books and their titles, authors and illustrators using books that learners are familiar with. Discuss how the cover of a book can tell the reader what the book is about. Using a selection of books, invite learners to say what the books might be about by looking at their covers.

Highlight 'Who' and 'What' questions before learners do the activity. Recap 'What' questions (see Unit 1) by asking questions. For example:

- What is the name of your school?
- What is the name of the road where you live?

Then ask learners some 'Who' questions

and elicit that the answer will be a name.

For example:

- Who brought you to school today?
- Who drew the picture?
- Who left the door open?

Now ask learners to look at the picture of the cover of *Max Can Do It!* on page 11 and answer questions 1–4.

Answers
1 Max Can Do It!
2 Learners' own answers.
3 Charlotte Raby
4 Sam Hearn

Reading and listening

1 Read the story to the class (pages 12–14).

Tell learners that you are going to read the story again. This time, while they listen, they need to think about these two questions:

- What did Bee like doing?
- What did Max like doing?

Ensure that they understand before reading the story again by asking them what they need to think about whilst they listen to the story.

When learners have read the story, invite them to say what Bee likes doing and what Max likes doing.

Workbook page 10

Reading and writing

Following on from working in pairs to discuss things they can and cannot do and their favourite things, learners complete a chart about these things. If necessary, teach the words in the chart and explain what rows and columns are in order to make reference to charts simpler. (Rows are horizontal (across) and columns are vertical (up and down).)

Make sure learners understand how to complete the chart before they start by asking them to point to where they will draw:

- their favourite thing at school
- their partner's favourite thing at school
- something they can do.

Student's Book page 15

Reading and speaking

Spend as much time as necessary on this section to ensure correct decoding of the text and to encourage reading with fluency. Encourage learners to use a variety of strategies, for example, phonic skills, picture and context clues, reading on and rereading, to work out any unknown words.

Draw the class together and invite individual learners to read aloud.

Observe and listen to learners as they discuss the text and talk about what the characters like doing. Check that they speak clearly and audibly and that they are aware of the listener.

Support: Some learners will need teacher support, individually or as part of a small group, to use these strategies. Support them by voicing the strategies they should use:

- What does the word start with?
- Let's try and sound the word out.
- Look at the picture. Does the picture help?
- Let's try reading from the beginning again.

Be careful not to allow the reader to become frustrated; read along with them and supply any word they are having difficulty with. Then ask them to read the sentence on their own.

Vocabulary: action words

Before asking learners to do activities 1 and 2, spend some time looking at words like 'cook' – 'cooking' and 'wish' – 'wishing'. Ask learners what they notice about the words in each pair.

You could make flash cards for pairs of words, for example, 'look' and 'looking'; 'crash' and 'crashing'; 'shout' and 'shouting'; 'cook' and 'cooking'; 'wish' and 'wishing'. Put the flashcards in random order on the board and ask learners to put them in pairs: a root word together with the corresponding word + –ing. (At this stage, learners are not expected to know terms like 'root word'. The activity is a simple matching one.)

Then ask learners: 'What do you notice about the words in each pair? How are they different from one another?'

Give learners opportunities to add –ing to given words, for example 'sleep', and have them say what the new word would be. Write the –ing word on the whiteboard, emphasising the –ing by circling it or underlining it.

At this stage, the list of words used should consist only of root words that do not change when –ing is added, for example: 'spell',

'cook', 'rain', 'brush', 'dust', 'bend', 'smell' and 'ring'.

Answers
2 Bee; Max; Max; Bee

Workbook page 11

Reading and writing

Ask learners to work in pairs to read the instructions for activities 1–3. To check understanding, ask one pair to say what they have to do.

Draw learners' attention to the heading on this page: *Reading and writing*. These are words that appear regularly and learners should recognise the common word ending –ing. At this point, the words are for reading recognition only. (Note: 'Writing' has a different spelling pattern.)

Give learners some time to do the activities independently, monitoring as they do so.

Answers
1 Max likes looking for things.; Max likes plodding in the mud.; Max likes looking at bugs.
2 looking; crashing; swinging; plodding; shouting; hunting; looking

Workbook page 12

Reading and writing

This section gives further practice in identifying words ending in –ing and reading them in the context of *Max Can Do It!* Learners' decoding of a familiar text is assessed, and their understanding of the story.

Learners match the beginnings of sentences with their endings.

Support: Support learners who may have difficulty with decoding, and assess their understanding of the story.

Answers
1 Bee had fun shouting and hunting.; Max had fun looking for things.; Max had fun plodding in the mud.; Bee had fun crashing in the trees.
2 Max went to swim in a deep pool.; Max sprang up and out of the pool.; Bee had got stuck up a tall tree.; Max got a ladder.

Extension: Use PCM 10 to reinforce the use of the ending –ing.

Weekly review

Use this rubric to assess learners' progress as they worked through the activities this week.

Level	Reading
■	This group can read the story and recognise sight words but does not consistently apply strategies for decoding unfamiliar words. With support they are making progress.
●	This group can read the story and recognise sight words but do not consistently apply strategies for decoding unfamiliar words. They used context well to work out –ing words.
▲	This group can read the story confidently on their own and use a range of strategies to decode words they do not know. They read words ending in –ing well.

Week 2

Student's Book pages 16–18

Workbook pages 13–14

Student's Book page 16

Spelling: high frequency words

Take every opportunity to help learners to identify, read and learn to spell words from the list of high frequency words. Use the 'look, say, cover, write and check' method as one of your strategies.

Learners need to get into the habit of looking at words with intent: observing details, highlighting difficult parts and visualising and committing the word to memory. Learners with poor visual memories may need extra support and practice to commit words to memory successfully.

1 Here learners are asked to scan pages of text to find high frequency words. Tell them that they do not have to read every word on the page; instead they should look for the words in a systematic way. For example:
1) They put a piece of card or a ruler under the first line of text. 2) They move their eyes from left to right and stop and point to an identified word if it appears on that line. 3) They then move the card/ruler to the next line of text and repeat the process.

Give learners practice in this skill before moving to the activity.

Support: Learners who struggle with this task could work in pairs to find the words.

As a follow-up, ask learners to practise looking at the words and identifying any tricky part. For example, in 'was' learners might think the vowel sound should be represented by the letter o. They should practise writing the words from memory.

2 This activity gives practice in using high frequency words to complete sentences about Max and Bee.

Answers
1 *the:* pages 1, 3, 4, 8, 11, 12
in: pages 1, 3, 4, 7
was: pages 2, 3
said: pages 4, 6, 9, 10, 11, 12
2 was; out; they; the

Student's Book page 17

Speaking and writing

In this section learners are given an opportunity to talk about what learners do to help others. Draw the class together to discuss how they themselves help others.

Extension: After a short discussion about doing things that are wrong or dangerous, for example, stealing or playing on or near railway lines, learners could choose a topic and do a short oral presentation about why they should not do these things. Monitor how clearly learners speak and how well they choose words to express themselves.

Sounds and spelling

This section focuses on x as a final sound in words, and on rhyming words that end in –ix, –ox and –ax.

Before learners do the activities, give them some practice in rhyming words by asking questions. For example: 'Who can tell me a word that rhymes with 'hat' / 'bed' / 'fit' / 'lot' / 'mix'?'

Support: For some learners, it may be necessary to say things like: 'I'm thinking of a word that starts with *m* and rhymes with "can".'

Using 'Max' and 'Rex' as examples, ensure that learners know how to write the letter that represents the sound at the end of both words (*x*).

Answers
1 Max – wax; box – fox; Rex
2 fix – mix – six; wax – tax – Max; box – fox

Workbook page 13

Reading and writing

1 Learners complete the sentences to say if they can or cannot do what is illustrated in the pictures.

2 They are then asked to write about what they can do to help someone.

Support: If learners are struggling to think of ways they could help someone, give them specific situations to write about. For example: 'A small child is lost at the supermarket. What could you do to help? Your mother is struggling to carry some heavy bags upstairs. What could you do to help?'

Extension: Learners work independently or in pairs to make a visual display to illustrate ways of helping others. They could draw pictures of themselves helping others and then write a caption underneath.

Support: It may be necessary to scribe for some learners. Ask them to say what their picture is about and then write for them: 'I am helping …'

Student's Book page 18

Sounds and spelling

This section asks learners to write consonant-vowel-consonant (CVC) words in rhyming pairs.

Before learners do the activity, give them some practice in identifying rhyming words. The examples below are oral activities and learners should focus on listening for sounds at the end of words.

Example 1: Read a rhyme emphasising the rhyming words.

> Becky Bee is busy,
> As busy as can be.
> She buzzes round the bushes
> And bangs into a tree.
>
> She bumps poor Boris Beetle
> When she bounces on his back,
> So Boris Beetle beetles off
> And hides beneath a sack.

Ask learners which words rhyme in the poem ('be' and 'tree'; 'back' and 'sack').

Example 2: Ask learners which two words sound the same at the end – in other words, which words rhyme.

Suggested words:

- 'flag', 'bag', 'box'
- 'three', 'flower', 'bee'
- 'goat', 'clock', 'sock'
- 'big', 'dig', 'path'
- 'fire', 'tyre', 'book'
- 'meat', 'seat', 'bench'
- 'car', 'house', 'jar'.

Remind learners that the rhyming words in the activity must sound the same at the end; when they write the words, only the first letter of each pair will be different, for example, 'bat' and 'hat'.

Note: 'Rhymes' and 'rimes' are not the same thing. Rhymes have word endings which sound the same but are not necessarily spelled in the same way, for example, 'socks' and 'fox'. Rimes are word endings which always retain the same spelling pattern, for example, 'box' and 'fox'.

Writing

The focus of this section is the use of capital letters at the beginning of names.

1 Learners are asked to write a list of the names of six people in the class. Remind them that the names need to be written in a list. Recap, if necessary, how to write a list.

Extension: More able learners could write other names, such as the days of the week or months of the year, forming the letters correctly and using a capital letter at the beginning of each name.

Answers
hat – cat;   bin – pin;   pen – hen;   hut – nut;
frog – log

Workbook page 14

Sounds and spelling

In this section learners write consonant-vowel-consonant (CVC) words and then write the words in rhyming pairs.

'Shop' and 'ship' are included on this page and it is necessary to have a teaching session about *sh* before learners do the activities. Tell learners to listen to the words 'shop' and 'ship' and say what sounds they hear in each word (*sh-o-p* and *sh-i-p*). **Note:** There are four letters in each word but only three sounds.

Tell learners that sometimes two letters join together to make one sound. *S* (the name of the letter) and *h* (the name of the letter) join together to make the sound *sh*. Show learners how to write *sh* and write the word 'shop' on the whiteboard. Do the same for the word 'ship'.

Ask learners to tell you words that begin with *sh*. Suggest a few words if necessary, for example, 'shoe' and 'shell'.

Move on to say pairs of words. Learners have to listen very carefully because the sounds at the beginning can sound alike. For example: 'Which words start with *sh*: 'shoe' or 'sock' / 'soup' or 'shop' / 'shell' or 'sell'?'

Tell learners that *sh* is not always found at the beginning of words. Ask them where they hear *sh* in words like 'dish', 'fish' and 'wash'. Give learners practice in identifying where they hear the *sh* sound: at the beginning or end of a word. **Suggested words:** 'shop', 'fish', 'shed', 'wish', 'wash', 'shelf', 'shadow', 'shift', 'dish', 'rush'.

PCM 11 should be used now.

Answers

1 mug; ten; shop; pen; mop; zip; jug; ship
2 mug and jug;   ten and pen;   shop and mop;   zip and ship

Dictation: At this level, learners need to develop their writing skills at the same time as they learn to use sounds to write simple words. Use the phrases and sentences below as class dictation to help them develop these skills on a regular basis. To encourage listening and thinking skills, instruct learners to listen carefully with their pencils down. Initially, it may be necessary to repeat the phrase to help learners to memorise it before asking them to write it down. Use one or two phrases or sentences a day to reinforce the skills.

- A fat cat on a mat.
- A jug and a mug.
- A fox on a box.
- A pin in a tin.
- A hen in a shed.
- A hat in a shop.
- A fish on a dish.

Extension: Learners could illustrate some of the dictation phrases. More able learners could write their own phrases and illustrate them.

You may now wish to teach the class some more combinations of two letters making one sound – *ch*, *th* and *wh* – using the same strategies. Use PCMs 12–13 to do this.

Weekly review

Use this rubric to assess learners' progress as they worked through the activities this week.

Level	Reading	Writing
■	This group can read consonant-vowel-consonant words and words with *sh* at the beginning/end when words are in lists but need some support when words are in context.	This group can write consonant-vowel-consonant words and are making good progress with medial *e* and medial *i* in words. They can write words with *sh* at the beginning.
●	This group can read consonant-vowel-consonant words and words with *sh* at the beginning/end with accuracy.	This group can write consonant-vowel-consonant words, and words with *sh* at the beginning/end.
▲	This group can read consonant-vowel-consonant words and words with *sh* at the beginning/end with speed and accuracy.	This group can write consonant-vowel-consonant words, and words with *sh* at the beginning/end with accuracy.

Week 3

Student's Book pages 19–20

Workbook pages 15–17

Workbook page 15

Sounds and spelling: the alphabet

Before learners do activities 1 and 2, give them opportunities to practise writing capital letters using dictation.

Remind learners that the alphabet can be written with capital letters and with lower case (small) letters. Give some examples: *D – d, F – f, W – w,* saying 'capital/small' as you write. Point out that some capitals are the same shape as the small letters, only bigger. For example: *C – c, O – o, P – p, S – s, V – v, W – w, X – x, Y – y* and *Z – z*.

Let learners read the instructions on their own. Check that they understand what is being asked before they do the activities independently.

Answers
1 T, D, F, G, P, B, N, H, M, B, R, S, W, Z

Student's Book page 19

Reading and writing

This section focuses on the characters of Max and Bee.

Ask learners to read the story *Max Can Do It!* again. Then have a class discussion about the characters. Ask learners: 'Who are the characters in the story?' Then ask them to tell you the names of characters in other familiar books or television shows.

Discuss what the characters Max and Bee are like. What words would learners use to describe them? Try to elicit the words in the box in activity 1 and write them on the whiteboard. Then talk about what Max and Bee like to do.

1 Learners do activity 1. Check that they can read the words in the box.

2–3 Learners are asked to read sentences about Bee and then to write sentences about Max. Check that learners remember that they need to use a capital letter at the beginning of each sentence and a full stop at the end.

4 The focus of this activity is what the characters say in the story.

Using the text, ask learners to read identified pages and pick out the words that Max said. Point out the page references and explain to learners they will find the words that Max said on these pages. For example:

Max: "I cannot do that. I am not quick."

Learners then read pages that you will identify and say what Bee might have said. For example:

Bee: "I like shouting and hunting."

Encourage learners to speak the words in the voice of the character. Ask them if they think Bee would speak in the same voice as Max.

Learners then do activity 4.

Support: Some learners may need help to find the words in the text to complete the sentences and it may be necessary to act as the scribe.

Answers
4 "I cannot do that. I am not quick."; "I can do that."

Workbook page 16

Sounds and spelling

1 Max and Bee often liked doing two things at the same time: Max liked plodding *and* squelching. Bee liked shouting *and* hunting. Write the word 'and' on the whiteboard and ask learners to say two things they like doing using 'and'.

Learners write the word 'and' three times.

2 Here learners are asked to add initial sounds to 'and' to make new words.

Write *at* on the whiteboard. Tell learners that you want to write the word 'cat' and ask them what sound must go at the beginning of *at* to change it into 'cat'. Confirm that it is *c* and write *c* to complete the word. Repeat this for other words, for example: 'sat', 'mat', 'rat', 'fat', 'bat', 'hat' and 'pat'.

Write 'and' on the whiteboard and ask learners what sound is needed to change 'and' to 'hand'. Confirm *h* and complete the word. Then learners do activity 2.

3 Learners add initial sounds to 'end' to make new words.

Answers
2 band; hand; land; sand
3 send; bend; lend; mend

Workbook page 17

Sounds and spelling

This section focuses on two letters making one sound – *sh*.

1 Give learners opportunities to practise identifying the *sh* sound in words.

Ask learners to listen for the *sh* sound as you say 'Crash!' and 'Smash!' Ask:

• Is *sh* at the beginning of the word?

• Is *sh* at the end of the word?

Do the same with other words, for example: 'shin', 'ship', 'sheep', 'shallow', 'shore', 'crash', 'mash', 'wash', 'fish' and 'dish'.

Ask learners to write the letters *sh* a number of times with speed and accuracy to reinforce the pattern.

2–3 Check that learners know what to do in activities 2–3 and then ask them to do the activities.

Answers

2 shop, shed, shut, ship, shell have a *sh* sound at the beginning; dish, wish, rush, mash, fish, rash, hush have a *sh* sound at the end.
3 fish; shell; ship

Student's Book page 20

Reading and writing

In this section, learners need to identify words ending in *sh* and then write a list of rhyming words.

Ask learners to do activities 1 and 2.

Support: Encourage learners to make a set of illustrated flashcards to show the meanings of the different words. Ask them to underline the *sh* sound in a different colour.

Answers
2 cash; dash; flash; bash; gash; crash; mash; rash; smash; sash; trash

Role play

Encourage learners to speak like their character. Invite pairs to perform for the rest of the class.

Extension: Able learners could develop a different scenario for Max and Bee and role-play it.

Listening and speaking

Put learners in pairs and ask them to discuss:

• what new words they have learnt

• what happened to Max's character in the story. How did he change?

Then draw the class together and invite them to say what they have discussed in pairs.

Weekly review

Use this rubric to assess learners' progress as they worked through the activities this week.

Level	Listening and speaking
■	This group spoke well to the class about how Max's character changed in the story.
●	This group showed awareness of their audience and spoke confidently to the class about how Max's character changed in the story.
▲	This group showed awareness of their audience and spoke confidently to the class about how Max's character changed in the story.

End of unit assessment

Use PCM 14 to assess whether learners can read and follow instructions, and whether they can read sentences and sequence them to retell a familiar story. This activity is similar to the one completed at the end of Unit 1. Focus particularly on those learners who had difficulty reading and following instructions to make sure they can read and understand them this time round. Also check that learners who sequenced work incorrectly show some improvement this time. Record your observations as necessary.

Unit 3 Let's find out

Unit overview

The focus in this unit is on non-fiction books and information texts. Learners will learn to 'read' the covers of books (illustrations and titles) and to find out if a book might contain information they need.

Learners will have the opportunity to find information from both illustrations and text – lists, labels, signs and captions. They will also have the opportunity to join in with reciting rhymes and playing with language.

Reading	Writing	Speaking and listening
1R03 Identify separate sounds (phonemes) within words, which may be represented by more than one letter, e.g. *th, ch, sh*. 1R06 Use phonic knowledge to read decodable words and to attempt to sound out some elements of unfamiliar words. 1R08 Join in with reading familiar, simple stories and poems. 1R09 Know that in English, print is read from left to right and top to bottom. 1R10 Read a range of common words on sight. 1R11 Enjoy reading and listening to a range of books, drawing on background information and vocabulary provided. 1R16 Read aloud independently from simple books. 1Rx1 Read labels, lists and captions to find information. 1Rv1 Show awareness that texts for different purposes look different, e.g. use of photographs, diagrams. 1Rv2 Know the parts of a book, e.g. title page, contents.	1W03 Know that a capital letter is used for 'I', for proper nouns and for the start of a sentence. 1W04 Use knowledge of sounds to write simple regular words, and to attempt other words including when writing simple sentences dictated by the teacher from memory. 1Wa2 Use relevant vocabulary. 1Wa3 Record answers to questions, e.g. as lists, charts. 1Wa5 Write for a purpose using some basic features of text type. 1Wt1 Write a sequence of sentences retelling a familiar story or recounting an experience. 1Wp2 Compose and write a simple sentence with a capital letter and a full stop. 1Ws4 Recognise common word endings, e.g. *–s, –ed* and *–ing*.	1SL1 Speak clearly and choose words carefully to express feelings and ideas when speaking of matters of immediate interest. 1SL2 Converse audibly with friends, teachers and other adults. 1SL3 Show some awareness of the listener through non-verbal communication. 1SL4 Answer questions and explain further when asked. 1SL6 Take turns in speaking. 1SL7 Listen to others and respond appropriately.

Related resources

- Audio files: *FACT FILE: Foxes*; *Five little ducks*; *Lion*
- Slideshow 3: Let's find out
- Image 2: Contents page
- PCM 15: Phonics *ng*
- PCM 16: Phonics *ck*
- PCM 17: End of unit assessment

© HarperCollins*Publishers* Ltd. 2016

Introducing the unit

The unit could be introduced by discussing with learners how they can find different types of information. For example, how could they find out about ocean pollution, whales, natural disasters or local weather conditions?

Explain to learners that the internet allows most types of information to be stored and found online. However, when they cannot use the internet or the information is not clear enough, they may need to use other sources of information, for example: the people around them, newspapers, magazines and books. Ask learners to give examples of other sources of information, for example: train/bus timetables, platform information, recipe books, store directories and local maps.

Show learners images or display different sources of information (use the examples above as a starting point) and talk about who might use each type of information, why they would use it and when they might need it. Also talk about what problems might result if they cannot find the information they need.

Week 1

Student's Book pages 21–23

Workbook pages 18–19

Student's Book page 21

Listening and speaking

Before learners start the unit, use a selection of non-fiction books to talk about how the front cover of a book can tell the reader what the book is about. Discuss with learners what kind of books they are (non-fiction books), and that this kind of book is sometimes referred to as a factual or information book. Using a selection of non-fiction books, invite learners to suggest what they are about, for example: books about animals, transport, dinosaurs, a visit to the dentist, the doctor, the beach, and so on.

Then suggest a topic that you want to find out about, for example, different types of fruit, and ask a learner to choose a book that they think would be good for finding out about fruit. Discuss their choice and why or why not it would be suitable. Repeat this for other topics, choosing topics to suit the non-fiction books that are available in the classroom.

Before learners do the activity in this section, ask them to read the instructions and questions in pairs.

Highlight 'What' and 'Which' question words and ensure that learners know what is being asked of them. ('What' is used to ask about things or activities; 'Which' is used to ask someone to choose between a small number of options.)

Give learners time to work in pairs and to talk about what is being asked. Remind them to take turns to speak, and to listen carefully to what their partner is saying. Monitor while learners work in pairs before drawing the class together to check answers.

Reading and writing

Ensure that learners understand the activities in this section. They should be able to work out that they need to write the titles of the books shown. Make a selection of non-fiction books available in class for the second activity.

Answers

1 In the Forest; Animal Coats; Pet Cat, Big Cat
2 Learners' own answers.

Workbook page 18

Writing

Before learners do the activity, show them front covers of non-fiction books to start a discussion about titles. Titles of non-fiction books are usually short – sometimes only one or two words, for example, *ROBOTS* or *Top Dinosaurs*. Discuss the size and style of the print and the use of capital letters.

Then refer to some non-fiction books from the class library and invite learners to comment on how the titles are written. Make sure that all learners can look at the books so that they can get ideas from them.

Now ask learners to work individually to write titles for the books on Workbook page 18.

Student's Book page 22

Reading and speaking
Recap what information a reader can get from the pictures in a book.

1–2 Draw learners' attention to the pictures from the books and give them time to look at them carefully. Encourage them to look for detail.

Write words like 'beak', 'wings', 'webbed feet' and 'feathers' on the whiteboard. Learners then work in pairs to talk about the page of *Animal Coats* shown on Student's Book page 22.

Reading and writing
Learners can now use the information that they found out from the picture, text and discussion to do activities 1 and 2. Remind them to use a capital letter, a full stop and a piece of information about ducks in each sentence.

Student's Book page 23

Sounds and spelling
Use the sentence 'A duck has wings' to highlight words where two letters make one sound – *ng* in 'wings' and *ck* in 'duck'.

Focus on *ng* first and remind learners that sometimes two letters join together to make one sound – *ng*. Tell them that *ng* is a nasal sound and that words in English do not start with *ng*, but that *ng* often comes at the end of words.

Ask learners to tell you words with *ng* at the end. Write the words on pieces of paper/card and stick them on the board, for example: 'song', 'hang', 'ding', 'lung'. Draw learners' attention to the fact that the words all have different vowels and *ng* at the end. Ask them to select words with the *–ing* rhyme from the words on the board and put them in a list so that the rhyme is easily seen. Then ask learners to read the *–ing* words.

Learners repeat the procedure to find rhymes with *ang* and *ong*.

Dictate words with *ang* and *ong* for learners to write.

Suggested words: 'king', 'bang', 'gang', 'fang', 'gong', 'ring', 'hang', 'sang', 'sing', 'song', 'wing', 'rang', 'ding', 'dong', 'thing'

Use PCM 15 at this stage to reinforce the phonics work around the *ng* sound.

Repeat the procedure for the sound represented by *ck*.

Suggested words: 'kick', 'rack', 'lick', 'pick', 'back', 'sack', 'sick', 'tick', 'tack', 'pack', 'dock', 'suck', 'neck', 'lock', 'deck', 'duck', 'luck', 'peck', 'rock', 'sock'

Use PCM 16 at this stage to reinforce the phonics work around the *ck* sound.

Learners do the activities on page 23 in the Student's Book once they have mastered the sounds.

1–2 Learners look at the pictures, say the words for each picture and write the words with *ng* at the end. They then write three rhyming words ending in *–ing*.

3–4 Learners look at the pictures, say the words for each picture and write the words with *ck* at the end. They then write lists of rhyming words ending in *–ock, –uck* and *–ack*.

Answers
1 wing; king; ring
2 ding; sing; ping
3 duck; sock; sack
4 dock, luck, back; lock, suck, rack; rock, tuck, pack

Workbook page 19

Sounds and spelling
This section gives further practice in writing words with *ng* or *ck* at the end.

These sentences can be used for dictation in this unit:
- Mum has a ring.
- My sock is on the bed.
- I can pack my bag.
- I sang a song.
- The sack is on my back.

Extension: Learners could investigate, read and spell words ending in *–ss, –ff* and *–ll*. They need to know the rule that consonant-vowel-consonant words do not end in *–s, –f* or *–l*, with the exceptions of 'gas', 'bus', 'has' and 'his'. (**Note:** The *s* in 'has' and 'his' sounds like *z*.)

Suggested words: 'mess', 'kiss', 'pass', 'toss', 'boss', 'less', 'miss', 'lass', 'loss', 'moss', 'hiss', 'mass', 'doll', 'cuff', 'bell', 'till', 'pill', 'huff', 'fell', 'bill', 'will', 'muff', 'tell', 'fill', 'ill', 'puff', 'sell', 'hill', 'well'

Answers
sock; sing; track; crack; truck; gong; swing; lock; ring

Weekly review

Use this rubric to assess learners' progress as they worked through the activities this week.

Level	Reading	Writing
■	This group can use pictures and, with support, text to find information. They are making good progress at reading words ending in *ck* and words ending in *ng*.	This group can spell words ending in *ck* and words ending in *ng* when words are dictated in a rhyming pattern.
●	This group can use pictures and text to find information. They can read words ending in *ck* and words ending in *ng*.	This group can spell words ending in *ck* and *ng* when words are dictated individually, and most of the time when the words are embedded in sentences.
▲	This group can use pictures and text to find information. They can confidently read words ending in *ck* and words ending in *ng*.	This group can spell words ending in *ck* and *ng* when words are dictated individually and in sentences.

Week 2

Student's Book pages 24–27

Workbook pages 20–21

Student's Book page 24

Reading, speaking and writing
The focus of this section is getting information from pictures and using it for a purpose. Learners are asked to write a sentence about a deer, a fox, a bat and an owl.

1 Here learners are asked to think what animals would be found in a forest. Draw the class together to clarify if the animals suggested would be found in a forest.

2 Here learners are asked to draw and label a forest animal. Before learners do the activity, talk to them about how to label a picture: the label should be close to the part of the animal that they are naming. Demonstrate with a drawing of your choice.

3 Learners work in pairs to discuss the information they can get from pictures of four forest animals. Monitor how learners take turns to speak and listen to their partner.

4 Before learners do activity 4, discuss the information that learners got from the pictures in activity 3 and write key words/phrases on the whiteboard. Using an owl as an example, write 'fly', 'wings', 'beak', 'nocturnal' and 'eyes at the front of the face'.

Model writing a sentence about a deer, a fox, a bat or an owl before asking learners to think about the sentences they could write. Invite some examples. Before learners write, ask them what they must remember when writing a sentence.

Student's Book page 25

Reading and writing
Before learners turn to page 25, show them contents pages from a few non-fiction books from the class library. Then show them a contents page and demonstrate how it is used.

Highlight that, unlike story books, non-fiction books do not need to be read from beginning to end and discuss why this is the case. Explain that a contents page can help the reader to find specific information without them having to read the whole book. For example:
• What would you find out about on page 14?
• What would you find out about on page 8?

Now ask learners to read the instructions and look at the contents page in activity 1 in the Student's Book. They then answer the questions in activity 2.

Answers
2 page 4; page 10; foxes in the city;
a fox's home

40

Student's Book page 26

Reading and speaking

Ask learners to work in pairs and give them time to read the fact file. Encourage them to look at the illustrations and to get as much information as possible from them before reading the text. Remind them that using information from illustrations along with other strategies, for example, initial sounds, can help them to work out unknown words.

Support: Support learners who may find the decoding more difficult by looking at the pictures with them and showing how the pictures can help with reading. For example, ask learners to look at the pictures of the food that foxes like to eat. Then ask them to identify the 'foods' and ask them what sound 'worm' starts with. Ask learners if they can find the word that says 'worms' (the word that starts with *w*) in the section of text about what foxes like to eat. Use the other pictures in a similar way to help learners to read the text.

Draw the class together to read the text, inviting some learners to read aloud. Then discuss what learners have found out about foxes. Ask some questions, for example:

- Where do foxes live?
- When do foxes go out?
- What is a baby fox called?
- What do foxes eat?
- What family of animals does the fox belong to?

Workbook page 20

Reading and writing

Discuss with learners what a fox looks like (learners can refer to previous pictures) and elicit the words that are needed to do the activity: 'long bushy tail', 'large ears', 'black eyes', 'sharp claws', 'fur' and 'pointed snout'.

Tell learners that when they label the parts of the fox, they need to write the name of the animal part in the box that has a line to that particular part.

Student's Book page 27

Reading and writing

1 Ask learners to read the fact file about foxes on page 26 again before they answer the questions. Check that all learners can read and understand the questions.

2–4 Before learners do activities 2, 3 and 4 discuss different ways of finding out information, for example: by looking in books, magazines and leaflets; by watching factual programmes on television; by looking at maps and timetables; by searching for information on the internet; or just by asking someone. It is important to have some of these sources of information available to show what information can be found and where, for example, what time a train leaves the station or what different types of bicycles are available in a certain shop.

Ask learners where they could look to find out what young animals are called and help them to find the answers.

Answers

1 a den; (any three of the following:) berries, worms, spiders, mice, birds; from bins; the dog family; a cub
3 camel – calf; sheep – lamb; tiger – cub
4 cub

Workbook page 21

Reading and writing

Before asking learners to do the activity, discuss with them what a fox, an owl, a bat and a deer look like. Discuss similarities and differences.

Show learners how to complete the chart. Tell learners to do the following:

- Read the words in the top row – the names of the animals.
- Read the words down the left-hand side (in the left column) – the names of animals' parts.
- Starting with 'fox', read the words going down on the left and stop when you come to a part that a fox has, in other words, 'legs'. This one has been done for you.
- Continue to read the words. 'Does a fox have wings? A beak? Feathers? Antlers? A tail?' When the answer is 'yes', put a tick in the box under 'fox' and in the same line as 'tail'.

Then choose another animal and work together with learners to check that they know what to do. Ask learners to complete the rest of the chart themselves.

Support: Some learners may need support to coordinate reading along the top row and down the left-hand column and finding the correct box to put the tick in. A piece of card placed so that learner can only read about the fox will help here. Help learners to position the card and then to move it along when they are ready to work out where to put the ticks for the owl, and so on.

Weekly review

Use this rubric to assess learners' progress as they worked through the activities this week.

Level	Reading
■	This group can record answers to questions on a chart when they have help with organisational skills.
●	This group can record answers to questions on a chart with minimal support.
▲	This group can confidently record answers to questions on a chart.

Week 3

Student's Book pages 28–30

Workbook pages 22–23

Student's Book page 28

Reading and writing

1 In this activity learners need to use information from photographs with labels to write three sentences about cats.

Before learners write the sentences, discuss the pictures and what information learners can get from them. Ask a learner to read question 2. Discuss what is meant by 'cat family'. Remind learners about the fox and ask what family the fox belongs to.

Then ask learners to say a sentence about a cat using the information they have been talking about.

2 In this activity learners look at pictures with labels and make a list of animals that belong to the cat family. Ask learners how to write words in a list before they do the activity.

Extension: Learners could add other animals to the cat and/or dog family.

Answers
2 lion, tiger, leopard, cheetah

Workbook page 22

Reading

Here learners are expected to complete a word search to reinforce animal vocabulary.

Before they do the activity, show them how to do a word search. Explain to learners that the words can go across the page or down the page and demonstrate by running your finger along and then down. Tell them that when they find a word in the word search, they should cross out this word in the box at the top. The first word, 'lion', has been found. Point out how the letters are arranged down the page and where the 'circle' has been drawn. Ask what should be done next – cross the word 'lion' out in the box at the top. Demonstrate another word in the same way and then ask learners to complete the word search.

Support: Some learners could work in pairs. Model the procedure with them if necessary.

Student's Book page 29

Reading and writing

Read the rhyme with learners. Then give them the opportunity to read out loud alone. Talk about what is happening in the rhyme and ask learners to predict what the next verse might be. ('Four little ducks went swimming one day', and so on.)

1 Ask learners to read the rhyme again and find the answers to the questions. They then write the pairs of rhyming words in the rhyme. Learners could learn the rhyme and recite it to their peers.

Extension: Learners could write the second verse of the rhyme, modelling it on the first verse.

2 This activity involves recognising the common word ending *–s* when s is added to a word to make the plural form.

42

Before turning to the activity, write pairs of words on the whiteboard. For example: 'dog – dogs', 'cup – cups', 'bed – beds', 'bag – bags', 'ring – rings', 'song – songs', 'sack – sacks', 'lock – locks'.

At this stage, only use words where the plural is formed by adding *s* to the root word.

Ask learners what they notice about the pairs of words and to explain why they are different. The first word in each pair is used to speak about one thing, for example, one dog or one ring. The second word in each pair is used to talk about more than one thing, for example, two beds, three locks or four cups.

Ask learners to write the plural form of words.

Suggested words: 'hat', 'cup', 'fan', 'tin', 'mug', 'bag', 'van', 'net', 'zip', 'tub', 'hens'

Learners then complete activity 2.

Answers
1 five;   day – away; quack – back
2 one duck; four frogs;   three cats;   five bats; two birds

Student's Book page 30
Reading and listening

This section involves reading and enjoying a poem about a lion.

Read the poem with learners and then talk about the words the author uses and why he chose them. Discuss what the words mean and how they make the reader feel about the lion.

Learners then complete activities 2–4.

Answers
3 roars – jaws;   quivers – shivers

Workbook page 23
Reading
In this activity, learners need to use what they have learnt about ducks and lions. They make sentences about ducks and sentences about lions. Ask learners to do the activity.

Answers
Ducks have feathers.   Ducks have beaks.
Ducks are birds.   Ducks have webbed feet.
Lions live in the jungle.   Lions roar.   Lions belong to the cat family.   Lions can run fast

Weekly review

Use this rubric to assess learners' progress as they worked through the activities this week.

Level	Reading	Writing
■	This group can confidently read labels and captions supported by illustrations in order to find information.	This group understand the concept of writing information in a list and, with some support, can write lists for a purpose.
●	This group can read labels and captions to find information.	This group understand the concept of writing information in a list and can write lists for a purpose.
▲	This group can read labels and captions to find information confidently.	This group fully understand the concept of writing information in a list and can write lists for a purpose.

End of unit assessment

The Workbook activity on page 23 can be used together with PCM 17 as an assessment of the skills learnt in this unit.

Unit 4 The moon

Unit overview

As learners work through this unit, they will read a story aloud and then retell and talk about the events in the story. *Bot on the Moon* is a simple fantasy story.

The unit could be part of a study about the sun, moon and stars.

Learners will have opportunities to read words with final and initial adjacent consonants by blending letters. They will also practise segmenting the words to spell them.

They will have opportunities to read and write high frequency words and other familiar words.

Reading	Writing	Speaking and listening
1R05 Blend to read, and segment to spell, words with final and initial adjacent consonants, e.g. *b–l*, *n–d*.	1Wa2 Use relevant vocabulary.	1SL3 Show some awareness of the listener through non-verbal communication.
1R06 Use phonic knowledge to read decodable words and to attempt to sound out some elements of unfamiliar words.	1Wt1 Write a sequence of sentences retelling a familiar story or recounting an experience.	1SL6 Take turns in speaking.
1R08 Join in with reading familiar, simple stories and poems.	1Wa3 Record answers to questions, e.g. as lists, charts.	1SL7 Listen to others and respond appropriately.
1R09 Know that in English, print is read from left to right and top to bottom.	1Wt1 Write a sequence of sentences retelling a familiar story or recounting an experience.	1SL4 Answer questions and explain further when asked.
1R10 Read a range of common words on sight.	1Wp1 Mark some sentence endings with a full stop.	
1R12 Make links to own experiences.	1Wa5 Write for a purpose using some basic features of text type.	
1R13 Retell stories, with some appropriate use of story language.	1Wa1 Write simple storybooks with sentences to caption pictures.	
1R16 Read aloud independently from simple books	1Ws3 Use rhyme and relate this to spelling patterns.	
1R17 Pause at full stops when reading.		
1R18 Identify sentences in a text.		
1Ri2 Talk about events in a story and make simple inferences about characters and events to show understanding.		
1Rw2 Recognise story elements, e.g. beginning, middle and end.		

Related resources:

- Slideshow 4: The moon
- Audio files: *Bot on the Moon*; *Mister Moon*
- PCM 18 Phonics: Adjacent consonants (consonant clusters) at the end of words
- PCMs 19–21 Phonics: Adjacent consonants (consonant clusters) at the beginning of words
- PCM 22 End of unit assessment

Introducing the unit

The unit could be introduced by discussing and listing places (real or imaginary) where learners would most like to go. After eliciting some initial ideas from learners, steer the discussion to an imaginary trip to the moon. Tell them that they are going to visit the moon and discuss the following questions with them.

- How would you get there?
- What might you take with you?
- What might you see?
- What might you do?

If learners are interested in the topic, extend this discussion and spend some time finding out about the moon and the conditions on it.

Week 1

Student's Book pages 31–35

Workbook pages 24–25

Workbook page 24

Reading and writing

In this section learners are asked to complete a dot-to-dot picture of a rocket using the lower case letters of the alphabet.

Revise alphabetical order by saying/singing alphabet rhymes with learners. (See page 9 of the Teacher's Guide.) It is useful to have an alphabet frieze displayed in the classroom for all learners to see. At this stage, many learners will need to be able to see the alphabet as well as hear it to aid learning.

Involve learners in a number of activities. For example:

- Say the name of a letter and ask a learner to find it on the alphabet frieze. Then ask: 'Is it near the beginning/near the end/in the middle of the alphabet?' Repeat for other letters.
- Recite the alphabet up to a certain letter, for example, recite 'a, b, c, d,' and invite learners to join in with the rest. Repeat for other parts of the alphabet.
- Give learners opportunities to practise giving the name of the next (or previous) letter in the alphabet. For example:

   Say 'b' and invite a learner to say what comes next. ('c')

   Say 'n' and invite a learner to say what comes next. ('o')

   Repeat for other letters of the alphabet.

Learners need to know the difference between the name of a letter and the sound that it represents. Ensure that you use the correct term – name or sound – when speaking to learners. Give practice to help with this. For example:

- Say the sound of a letter and ask learners to say the name.
- Say the name of a letter and ask learners to say the sound.

Student's Book pages 31–34

Reading and speaking

Ask learners to work with a partner and to look at the cover of *Bot on the Moon* and then read the text. When learners have read the text, draw the class together to check that their reading is correct and that they know what they are going to talk about.
Monitor as they talk, stepping in as necessary to keep learners on task and making sure that they speak audibly and without dominating the talk with their partner.

When learners have finished talking, draw the class together again and invite learners to give answers to the questions.

Answers
Bot on the moon; Shoo Rayner is the writer and illustrator; a fantasy story book; Bot; a robot; golf

Student's Book page 35

Reading and listening

Tell learners that you are going to read the story again. This time, while you read, they need to listen for two things. Ask learners to read the instructions and to say what they need to listen for.

Read the story again. Check that learners found the answers to the questions through listening.

Reading and writing

1 Learners read the story in pairs before reading it aloud. Praise good use of reading strategies and fluency.

Spend as much time as necessary on this section to ensure correct decoding of the text

45

and to encourage reading with fluency. Encourage learners to use a variety of strategies, for example, phonic skills, picture and context clues, reading on and rereading, to work out any unknown words.

After reading, ask questions to check understanding.

- How did Bot travel to the moon?
- What did Bot buy at the Moon Shop?
- Who did Bot send the postcard to?
- What did Bot lose?
- Did Bot get the club back?

2 Learners write answers to the questions.

3 In this activity, learners need to write the sentences that are true. Remind learners that they have done an activity like this before (in Unit 1). Say a few sentences and ask learners to tell you if they are true or false.

Answers
1 by rocket;   a card and a moon rock
2 fast;   a golf club
3 The moon had lots of hills.; Bot had lost his club.; The club hit Bot on his hat.

Workbook page 25
Reading and writing
1 Before learners do the activity, have a discussion about what Bot bought in the Moon Shop and what else he might have bought. Link to learners' own experiences of what they might buy as a souvenir when they visit a place of interest, for example: a poster, a T-shirt, sweets or a toy.

Ask learners to look at the picture of the shop window and to tell you the name of an item in the window. Ask them if they can think of anything else that could be for sale in the Moon Shop, for example: spare parts for rockets and clothes for travelling in a rocket.

2 Remind learners how a shopping list is written before they complete Bot's shopping list from items in the shop window.

Support: Work with individuals or groups to help them copy the names of the items accurately. Encourage the use of a 'marker' to keep the place of each word that learners copy. It can be difficult for some learners to move their eye from the word and then back to where they are writing without losing their place.

Extension:
1 Able learners might want to add items of their own to the shopping list.
2 Learners could draw or make items for a Moon Shop window display and then make labels for the items.

Weekly review

Use this rubric to assess learners' progress as they worked through the activities this week.

Level	Reading	Writing
■	This group read familiar text well but need support to tackle unfamiliar text.	This group can write a shopping list choosing from a number of given items.
●	This group read well and are becoming more confident about using strategies to tackle unfamiliar words.	This group can write a shopping list choosing from a number of given items and then add an item of their own.
▲	This group read well and use strategies independently to tackle unfamiliar words.	This group can write a shopping list choosing from a number of given items and then add items of their own.

Week 2

Student's Book pages 36–38

Workbook pages 26–28

Workbook page 26

Reading
This activity assesses learners' decoding of a familiar text and their understanding of the story. Learners match the beginning of sentences with their endings.

Answers
Bot zoomed past all the twinkling stars.; He sent the card to his mum.; Bot was back with Mum.; Bot was on a trip to the moon.; The club hit Bot on his hat.; Bot landed on the moon.

Student's Book page 36

Sounds and spelling
The activities in this section focus on reading words with final adjacent consonants and then writing words that rhyme with 'fast'.

1 Before learners do this activity, spend some time teaching them about adjacent consonants (consonant clusters) at the end of words. Tell them that there will be two sounds at the end of the words you are going to say and that they should listen carefully to hear both (*s* and *t* to make *st*).

Ask learners to identify the sounds at the end of the words 'fast', 'test', 'lost' and 'just'. Pronounce both consonants in the final consonant cluster carefully. (In everyday speech one of these often becomes dominant.)

Ask learners to read the sentence in the box and find the word 'fast'.

2 Say the word 'nest' slowly and clearly and ask learners how many sounds they can hear (four sounds). Ask one learner to write the word 'nest' on the whiteboard.

Repeat the procedure for other words, for example: 'fast', 'test', 'rust', 'last', 'must', 'mast', 'jest', 'past', 'west', 'just', 'best', 'pest' and 'dust'. Ask learners to write some of the words to dictation, reminding them that each word has four letters.

Once you have done this, you could do the same for words ending in *nt, lt* and *ft*.

Suggested words:
- 'went', 'tent', 'bent', 'sent', 'dent', 'lent', 'pant', 'mint', 'tint'
- 'melt', 'felt', 'belt', 'kilt', 'wilt', 'tilt'
- 'soft', 'loft', 'raft', 'gift', 'lift', 'left'.

Ask learners to complete activity 2.

Other consonant clusters that need to be taught using the same procedure are *lf, mp, nd, lk* and *sk.*

Suggested words:
- 'elf', 'self', 'shelf', 'golf'
- 'camp', 'damp', 'lamp', 'ramp', 'bump', 'dump', 'jump', 'hump', 'lump', 'limp'
- 'band', 'hand', 'land', 'sand', 'bend', 'lend', 'send', 'mend', 'pond', 'fond'
- 'milk', 'silk', 'bulk', 'hulk', 'sulk'
- 'ask', 'mask', 'task', 'risk', 'tusk', 'rusk', 'desk', 'tusk'.

These phrases can be used as dictation to check and test spelling in this unit:
- Junk on a bunk.
- A mint on a desk.
- Dust on a lamp.
- A vest in a nest.
- A bump and a jump.
- A hand in the sand.
- A nest in the loft.
- A mask on a shelf.
- A gift in a lift.

Use PCM 18 either as a reinforcement activity or to test skills in this area.

Answers
2 last;   past;   mast

Reading and writing
The focus of this section is the concept of a sentence – identifying sentences in a text and pausing at full stops when reading.

Give learners opportunities to highlight sentences in a familiar text. A good activity is to give learners a piece of copied text and highlighter pens. Then read a short sentence from the copied text for learners to find and highlight. Remind them to start highlighting at the beginning of the sentence (the capital letter) and to end at the full stop. They should then find and highlight another sentence using a different colour for each sentence.

Before learners do activities 1–4, ask them to read the questions aloud and check that they know exactly what is being asked.

Answers
2 three sentences
3 Bot;   The;   It

Workbook page 27

Sounds and spelling

Before learners do this activity, spend some time revising adjacent consonants (consonant clusters) at the end of words. Give them opportunities to identify adjacent final sounds in spoken words. Use some of the words from the guidance on teaching adjacent consonants (consonant clusters). Ask learners to write the two letters that represent the sounds they hear. Say the words clearly, with emphasis on the final adjacent consonants.

Ask learners to do the activity.

Answers
lk – milk; ft – raft; st – nest; nt – tent;
nd – hand; lf – golf; lt – belt; nd – pond;
st – vest

Student's Book page 37

Sounds and spelling

The focus of activity 1 is adjacent sounds at the beginning of words. Before learners do this activity, it may be necessary to spend some time teaching them about adjacent consonants (consonant clusters) at the beginning of words.

Tell learners that you are going to say words with two sounds at the beginning. They have to listen carefully to hear both sounds (*t* and *r*). Pronounce both consonants in the initial consonant cluster clearly. Say the word 'trip' slowly and ask learners to say how many sounds they can hear (four sounds). Ask a learner to write the word 'trip' on the whiteboard.

Repeat the procedure for other words: 'trap', 'trod', 'trim' and 'trot'. Ask learners to write the words to dictation reminding them that each word has four letters.

There are a number of adjacent consonants where the second consonant is *r*, for example: *br, cr, dr, fr, gr* and *pr*. Write the clusters *br, cr, dr, fr, gr, pr* and *tr* on cards on cards and stick the cards on the whiteboard. Tell learners that you will say a word and they need to say and point to the two letters that the word starts with.

Suggested words:

- 'bridge', 'brass', 'broom', 'brick', 'brush'
- 'crab', 'cry', 'crown', 'cross', 'crust'
- 'drawer', 'drip', 'dragon', 'drink', 'drum'
- 'friend', 'frog', 'frill', 'frock', 'fruit'
- 'grab', 'gran', 'grapes', 'grin', 'grass'
- 'pram', 'press', 'present', 'prize', 'pretty'
- 'train', 'truck', 'trailer', 'track', 'tractor'

Say some of the words above and ask learners to write the first two letters they hear in each word. Learners should not be asked to write the whole word at this stage.

PCM 19 can be used at this stage to reinforce the concepts.

Use the same procedure to teach other consonant clusters at the beginning of words, for example, *bl, cl, fl, gl, pl, sk, sl, sm, sn, sp, st* and *sw*.

PCMs 20 and 21 can be used to reinforce and assess the spelling of words with these consonant clusters.

Support: It can be difficult for some learners to hear the differences between clusters. Individual speech problems can also cause difficulties. Support and give additional practice.

Dictation: Use these sentences for dictation in this unit.

- Gran has a long dress.
- Greg has a plan.
- Brad has a drum.
- The pram is on the grass.
- The frog can swim.
- The fish is in the pond.
- Mum went to the bus stop.
- Glen can jump and skip.
- The plug is in the sink.
- The flag is on the cliff.
- The crab is on the sand.
- The desk has a flat top.

1 Learners are asked to say and write words with consonant clusters at the beginning of each word.

2 Here learners read high frequency words and use them to complete sentences. More than one word is missing from each sentence. Tell learners to read the whole sentence and decide which words are needed so that the sentence makes sense before they write. The word 'the' needs to be used twice.

Learners should have on-going practice in reading and writing high frequency words and use the 'look, say, cover, write and check' method for learning to spell the words.

3 Before learners do the activity, discuss what might be included in a picture postcard from the moon.

Answers
1 club; frog; flag; plug; drum
2 got; and; the; He; the; to; his

Workbook page 28

Reading and writing

This section involves completing sentences with words from *Bot on the Moon*. The words all have adjacent consonant sounds at the beginning of the word, at the end of the word, or both. There are no words for learners to copy, and whilst the purpose of the activity is to write the words from memory, it is important to ensure that learners know what words are missing. If necessary, allow them to work in pairs to read the sentences and work out the missing words together.

Support: Some learners may need to refer back to the text to find the correct word. Allow them to do this only after they have tried to work it out.

Answers
1 trip **2** Blast **3** fast **4** past **5** sent **6** trip

Student's Book page 38

Reading and writing

In this section learners are asked to read sentences and then to write them in the correct order. Encourage learners to use the pictures and to look for clues in the text to work out the order before they start writing.

For example: Bot got out the moon rock and his best golf club.

Question: What tells the reader that this is the first sentence?

Answer: Bot had to get the moon rock and his best golf club out *before* he could hit the moon rock.

After learners have finished writing, remind them to read the sentences they have written and check that the order makes sense. Allow them to work in pairs to check and assess each other's work. Peer assessment is an important and valuable tool for learning.

Support: The sentences could be copied and given to learners. This way they can manipulate the text until they get the correct order before they write the sentences themselves.

Answers
2 Bot got out the moon rock and his best golf club.; He hit the moon rock.; It was a big hit.; Bot let go of the club.

Weekly review

Use this rubric to assess learners' progress as they worked through the activities this week.

Level	Reading	Writing
■	This group can read words with consonant clusters at the beginning and at the end of words but need regular practice to improve accuracy.	This group can write words with consonant clusters when dictated as individual words.
●	This group can read words with consonant clusters at the beginning and at the end of words with accuracy.	This group can write words with consonant clusters when dictated as individual words and in sentences.
▲	This group can read words with consonant clusters at the beginning and at the end of words with speed and accuracy.	This group can write words with consonant clusters when dictated as individual words and in sentences. They spell them well in their own writing most of the time.

Week 3

Student's Book pages 39–40

Workbook page 29

Student's Book page 39

Speaking, reading and writing

1 Working in pairs, learners retell the story to each other. Monitor that they are taking turns to speak and listen and that they are telling the events of the story in the correct sequence.

Support: It may be necessary to support some learners by asking questions like 'What happened after that? What happened next?' and so on.

2 This activity asks learners to draw a story map to illustrate the story from 'Blast off!' to the point when Bot got a card at the Moon Shop. Discuss the main events in the sequence:

- The rocket went fast.
- It zoomed past the stars.
- It landed on the moon.
- Bot went up and down the hill.
- He got a card and a moon rock at the Moon Shop.

Tell learners that there should be five pictures, one for each part of the story on their story map. Talk with them about where their first picture should be positioned on the page and in what direction the pictures should go.

Extension: Ask learners to write a caption under one or more pictures. You will need to decide what is appropriate for individual learners.

3 Learners are asked to draw a robot and give it a name before writing a sentence about their robot.

Student's Book page 40

Listening, reading and writing
Mister Moon is a poem for learners to listen to, read and enjoy.

1 Read the poem to learners and then read it again while they follow the words. Then give them time to read it in pairs.

Take some time to discuss the poem and talk about how it is written. It is written in rhyming couplets, which are two lines of poetry of about the same length that rhyme. Rhyming words are words that sound the same when spoken but they do not necessarily have to be spelt the same.

Examples of rhyming couplets:

> It's hard to see the butter<u>fly</u>
> Because he flies across the <u>sky</u>.

> Lightning, thunder all <u>around</u>,
> Soon the rain falls on the <u>ground</u>.

2 Ask learners, in turn, to read aloud one of the rhyming couplets from the poem and to identify the rhyming words in the couplet that they read. They then write the rhyming words in pairs.

Learners should memorise the poem and recite it to their peers.

Answers
sky – eye; go – hello; see – me;
bright – night

Workbook page 29

Reading and writing
This section follows on from Student's Book page 40. Here learners complete each rhyming couplet by choosing the correct ending from those provided. Ask learners to read the poem again, and then check that they can read the poem endings before they do the activity.

Answers
with his big bright eye.; Mister Moon! Hello!; to follow me?; Mister Moon! Good night!

Weekly review

Use this rubric to assess learners' progress as they worked through the activities this week.

Level	Listening and speaking
■	This group can retell the events of a story but need some support to sequence them.
●	This group can retell a story with the events in sequence.
▲	This group speak clearly and can retell a story with the events in sequence.

End of unit assessment

Hand out PCM 22 and ask learners to complete it under test conditions to make sure they are able to deal with consonant clusters at the beginning and end of words.

Unit 5 Funny Fish

Unit overview

As learners work through this unit, they will read a story aloud and then retell and talk about the events in the story. *Funny Fish* is a story with patterned and predicable language. *A Fine Feathered Fish* is a nonsense rhyme.

The unit could be part of a study about how fish and sea animals protect themselves or the wider topic of camouflage in animals.

Learners will have the opportunity to develop an understanding of a group of letters that make one sound – *igh*.

They will also have opportunities to read and write high frequency words and other familiar words.

Reading	Writing	Speaking and listening
1R02 Know the name of and most common sound associated with every letter in the English alphabet.	1W03 Know that a capital letter is used for 'I', for proper nouns and for the start of a sentence.	1SL1 Speak clearly and choose words carefully to express feelings and ideas when speaking of matters of immediate interest.
1R05 Blend to read, and segment to spell, words with final and initial adjacent consonants, e.g. *b–l, n–d*.	1Wa2 Use relevant vocabulary.	
1R06 Use phonic knowledge to read decodable words and to attempt to sound out some elements of unfamiliar words.	1Wa3 Record answers to questions, e.g. as lists, charts.	
	1Wt1 Write a sequence of sentences retelling a familiar story or recounting an experience.	1SL2 Converse audibly with friends, teachers and other adults.
1R10 Read a range of common words on sight.	1Wp2 Compose and write a simple sentence with a capital letter and a full stop.	1SL3 Show some awareness of the listener through non-verbal communication.
1R14 Learn and recite simple poems.		
1R15 Join in and extend rhymes and refrains, playing with language patterns.	1Ws1 Begin to learn common spellings of long vowel phonemes, e.g. *ee, ai, oo*.	1SL6 Take turns in speaking.
1R16 Read aloud independently from simple books	1Ws2 Spell familiar common words accurately, drawing on sight vocabulary.	1SL7 Listen to others and respond appropriately.
1Ri2 Talk about events in a story and make simple inferences about characters and events to show understanding.	1Ws3 Use rhyme and relate this to spelling patterns.	1SL8 Listen carefully to questions and instructions.
1Rw2 Recognise story elements, e.g. beginning, middle and end.	1Ws4 Recognise common word endings, e.g. *–s, –ed* and *–ing*.	
1Rv2 Know the parts of a book, e.g. title page, contents.		

Related resources

- Slideshow 5: Funny Fish
- Audio files: *Funny Fish*; *A fine feathered fish*
- Image 3: *The Nut Tree*
- PCM 23: End of unit assessment

Introducing the unit

Introduce the unit by telling learners that they are going to read a book about fish. Explain that they are not fish that behave the way we think they do; they are fish that can talk.

Ask individual learners to tell the class about any films or programmes they have seen in which fish can talk. There are many such films and learners may have seen *Finding Nemo*, *Shark Tale* or *Help! I'm a Fish*.

Week 1

Student's Book pages 41–46

Workbook page 30

Student's Book pages 41–42

Reading and speaking

1 Read the instructions with learners. Then ask them to read the first part of the instructions with you. Ask:

- How many words are in this sentence?
- What is the last word in the sentence?
- What comes after the last word in the sentence?
- What word does the next sentence start with?
- What word does the next sentence end with?
- What do you notice about 'Look' and 'book'?

Give learners time to read what they are being asked to talk about, in pairs and individually, before inviting a learner to read aloud. Model correct reading and ensure that learners understand what is being asked of them before they do the activity. Monitor learners, ensuring that they talk about what has been asked, that they take turns to speak, and that they listen carefully when their partner speaks.

Then draw the class together for a discussion and check the points that they have discussed.

Move on to talk about the fact that the page is a title page. Ask:

- How does it differ from the cover of a book?
- Have you noticed the symbol and name at the bottom of the page?
- What does the symbol stand for? What about the name?

Talk briefly about how an author writes a book (the words of the book), and explain that the publisher then makes the physical book.

2 Read page 42 with learners, emphasising the rhythm. Encourage them to join in using the pattern of the text to support decoding.

Ask learners to look at the word 'swimming' – what do they notice at the beginning of the word? (the consonant cluster *sw*) Explain to learners that recognising *sw*, along with the context of the story, helps them to know what the word is. Draw their attention to the end of the word and ask what they notice. (It ends in –*ing*.)

Student's Book pages 42–45

Reading and writing

1 Let learners work in pairs to read page 42 of the story and predict what the story is going to be about. Learners use the picture to predict which fish said, "Look at me!"

Draw the class together to discuss what they have been talking about and to check understanding. Talk about the expressions on the faces of the fish and what those expressions tell the reader.

2 Read the rest of the story with learners, emphasising the rhythm, and encourage learners to join in using the pattern of the text to support decoding.

Ask learners to look at page 43 and to find another word starting with *sw* – 'swish'. Talk about why 'swish' is written three times and why there are three dots after the last 'swish'. Then ask learners to look at the word 'bright' on page 42 and model how to read it. Use phonic knowledge to tackle *br* and help learners to see how the context and the grammar of the sentence help to predict the word.

Spend as much time as necessary on this activity to ensure correct decoding of the text and to encourage reading with fluency. Encourage learners to use a variety of strategies – phonic skills, picture and context clues, reading on and rereading – to work out any unknown word.

Ask some questions to ensure understanding. For example:

- How many fish were swimming in the sea?
- Which fish was eaten first by the shark?
- What colour was the second fish to be eaten?
- Why wasn't the third fish eaten?

Look more closely at the word 'bright' and its spelling pattern with learners.

Reading the story provides an ideal opportunity for learners to read high frequency words in context and then to learn to spell them. This is something that can be done throughout the three weeks that it takes to cover this unit. Use the 'look, say, cover, write and check' method as one of your strategies.

Learners need to get into the habit of looking at words with intent: observing details, highlighting difficult parts, visualising and committing a word to memory. Learners with poor visual memories may need extra support and practice to commit words to memory successfully.

Learners can work in pairs and then individually to read the rest of the story again. Spend as much time as necessary on this section to ensure accurate decoding and to encourage reading with fluency.

Support: Support individuals and small groups when necessary while they are reading.

3 Learners are asked to say if sentences are true or false. Ask them to find evidence in the text for their answers. For example:

The fish were swimming in a pond.

False: The evidence for this is on page 1. The fish were swimming in the <u>sea</u>.

This is a good strategy for learners to begin to develop at this early stage, and you should check as you monitor that learners are using it.

Answers
3 One fish was red.; One fish hid under a stone.; The big fish ate two fish.; One fish was yellow like the sun.

Workbook page 30

Reading
This activity assesses learners' decoding of the now familiar text and their understanding of the story. They match the beginning of sentences with their endings.

Answers
Three funny fish were swimming in the sea.; I am bright and funny and red.; That was the end of the funny red fish.; I am yellow – as bright as the sun!; I can look like a stone.; The big bad fish leaves me alone!

Student's Book page 46

Reading and writing
Before learners do the activities in this section, have a discussion with them about the fish. Talk about words to describe the different fish, eliciting the words in activity 1: 'red', 'clever', 'brown', 'bossy', 'shy', 'bright', 'funny', 'boastful' and 'spotty'.

Ask learners to describe why the funny brown fish was saved from the shark. Introduce the word 'camouflage'. What other creatures use camouflage to hide in the wild? Use images of animals using camouflage. Ask why the red and yellow fish were eaten. Was it only because they were brightly coloured?

Read through activities 1–5 with learners, checking that they know what to do.

Show on the whiteboard how to set out the two lists for activity 2.

Ask learners where they will find the words to complete the sentences in activity 3.

For activity 4, talk with learners about what labels they should write on their pictures of fish and where to write them.

For activity 5, remind learners what you will be looking for in their written sentences.

Answers
2 red fish: red, bossy, bright, funny, boastful; brown fish: clever, brown, shy, spotty
3 Answers can include any two of the following: clever; brown; shy; spotty.
Answers can include any two of the following: red; bossy; bright; funny; boastful.

Weekly review
Use this rubric to assess learners' progress as they worked through the activities this week.

Level	Reading	Writing
■	This group are becoming more accurate with decoding and have a good understanding of what they read.	This group can draw and label their drawing.
●	This group read with increasing accuracy and have a good understanding of what they read.	This group can draw and label their drawing accurately.

| | This group read with increasing fluency and accuracy, and have a very good understanding of what they read. | This group can draw and label their detailed drawing accurately. |

Week 2

Student's Book pages 47–48

Workbook pages 31–33

Workbook page 31
Writing

Before learners do the activity, talk about the pictures and invite learners to say what they might write about. Encourage them to speak clearly, making what they say as interesting as possible. Then choose one learner's description of what is happening in the picture and model how to write it. Give a running commentary as you write, for example: 'I am starting with a capital letter because we always start sentences with a capital letter. I remember how to write 'fish' by sounding it out: *f-i-sh*. At the end of the word 'fish' there are two letters that make one sound.' Continue to voice where appropriate as you write. If necessary, ask another learner for their description and repeat the process.

Support: Work with a small group and invite each learner to say what they are going to write. Support them as they write. Scribe for individual learners if necessary. Learners could then write below your text.

Student's Book page 47
Reading and writing

This section focuses on reading and spelling familiar common words (words for the colours).

Tell learners that the words are all colour words and this should help them to read the words. Ask: 'How?' Then say: '"Blue", "black" and "brown" all start with *b* so how do we know which is which? We need to look at the next letter. *Br* helps with "brown" but "blue" and "black" both have *bl* at the beginning. What else? "Black" has a *c* sound at the end and "brown" has a *n* sound at the end.'

Remind learners that if they use two colour words in a sentence, they need to use 'and'.

Give learners opportunities to practise writing the colour words. They should look at a word and highlight any part of that word that they

find tricky. Think of what would help them to remember how to spell the word and get them to practise writing it.

Ask learners to do the activities.

Answers
3 The flower is yellow and red. / The flower is red and yellow.
The owl is brown and black. / The owl is black and brown.
The bird is blue and green. / The bird is green and blue.
The butterfly is purple and white. / The butterfly is white and purple.

Workbook page 32
Reading and spelling

This section focuses on finding high frequency words in the story and using them to complete sentences.

Some learners may be able to scan the text to find if the words appear on the pages. A useful strategy is to place a 'marker' underneath the first line of print and pull it down as they read each line of print. Other learners will need to focus on more detailed reading. Again a 'marker' would be beneficial.

Remind learners that when they are looking for certain words in the story, they do not need to read every word.

Learners do activities 1 and 2.

Answers
1 *said*: pages 2, 4, 8, 10, 12
came: pages 5, 9, 11
were: pages 1, 7
was: pages 6, 10,
Then: pages 5, 9, 11
2 came; said; were; was; Then

Student's Book page 48
Sounds and spelling

This section focuses on the word 'bright' in the text and uses rhyme to relate it to the spelling pattern *ight*.

Before learners do the activities, use the word 'bright' as a starting word as it is a word they

54

have read in the story. Ask learners what sounds they hear: *b-r-igh-t*. There are four sounds in the word 'bright'.

Ask learners to look at the word 'bright' in their books. Remind them that sometimes more than one letter makes one sound. Ask them If they can work out which letters make the long *i* sound. Confirm that the letters are *igh*. Write the word 'bright' on the whiteboard with learners' help by asking which letter comes first, second, and so on.

Now use onset and rhyme to write other words ending in *–ight*. Point to the word 'bright' on the whiteboard and ask learners what word they would get if they changed *br* for *fr* and then for *fl*. Draw their attention to the consonant clusters at the beginning of these words.

Repeat the procedure with the words 'fight', 'light', 'might', 'night', 'right' and 'sight'.

Tell learners that this is only one way to write the long *i* sound and that they will learn about others at another time.

1 Ask learners to practise writing the group of letters *igh* for speed and accuracy. They then do activity 1.

2 Learners use some of the *ight* words to complete and then copy sentences.

Dictation: Here are some sentences that are suitable for dictation in this unit.

- I might go to the shops.
- I went to bed last night.
- The sun is bright.
- I cut my right hand.
- The big light is on.

Answers
1 fright; light; fight; night; sight; might; right; tight; flight
2 light; night; bright; right

Workbook page 33
Sounds and spelling
This section focuses on words with adjacent consonants and the vowels of the words. Learners change the vowel sound to make new words.

Ask learners to say, 'Angry elephants in orange underwear' to remind them of the vowels – *a, e, i, o* and *u*.

Ask learners to say the sounds of the vowels and then the names of the vowels in sequence. A good aid is to spread the fingers of one hand and point to each finger in turn as you say the words 'Angry elephants in orange underwear' or *a, e, i, o, u* (names and sounds).

Give learners practice in changing the vowel sounds in words to make new words. Use a word like 'lift'. Say: 'Change the vowel to *e*. What word will it be?' ('left')

Repeat the procedure with 'fast' ('fist'), 'must' ('mist'/'mast'), 'land' ('lend'), 'limp' ('lamp'/'lump') and 'sink' ('sank'). For this activity learners could use whiteboards to write the words, or magnetic letters.

Learners then do the activity in the Workbook.

Answers
rust; lump; send; pest; last; damp; band; loft

Weekly review

Use this rubric to assess learners' progress as they worked through the activities this week.

Level	Reading	Writing
■	This group can read words with the long vowel *i* represented by *igh* when the words are in rhyming lists.	This group can write simple sentences with a capital letter and a full stop. They often need a model to spell familiar common words.
●	This group can read words with the long vowel *i* represented by *igh* with accuracy. They recognise and read them when the *igh* word is embedded in text.	This group can write simple sentences with a capital letter and a full stop. They can spell some familiar common words accurately.
▲	This group can read words with the long vowel *i* represented by *igh* with speed and accuracy. They recognise and read them when the *igh* word is embedded in text.	This group can write simple sentences with a capital letter and a full stop. They can spell familiar common words accurately.

Week 3

Student's Book pages 49–50

Workbook pages 34–35

Student's Book page 49

Reading

A Fine Feathered Fish is a nonsense rhyme for learners to read and enjoy.

Read the rhyme to learners with expression before asking them to join in reading. Take some time to discuss the poem, its content, the alliterative language and its rhyming pattern. Ask some questions, for example:

- How many fins did the furry fish have?
- What happened to the fine feathered fish?
- Why do you think the fine feathered fish yelled to the fish in the tins?
- What do you notice about some of the words/lines in the poem? (Some words rhyme; some words start with the same letter; two lines are the same.)

Learners should memorise the rhyme and recite it to their peers.

Workbook page 34

Reading and writing

Learners complete the poem by selecting the correct endings for lines. Encourage learners to read the poem again after they have completed the activity to check that it reads correctly.

Answers

five furry fins; four fishy tins.; five furry fins; out of those tins!

Student's Book page 50

Reading and writing

1 In this activity learners read the poem and then choose the correct words to complete sentences about the poem.

2–3 Before learners do activities 2 and 3, give them the opportunity to listen to and read some rhyming poems. Start with *Nut Tree* by Julia Donaldson, showing learners the text.

Nut Tree
by Julia Donaldson

Small, brown, hard, round,
The nut is lying underground.

Now a shoot begins to show,
Now the shoot begins to grow.

Tall, taller, tall as can be,
The shoot is growing into a tree.

And branches grow and stretch and spread
With twigs and leaves above your head.

And on a windy day
The nut tree bends, the branches sway.

The leaves fly off and whirl around,
And nuts go tumbling to the ground.
Small, brown, hard and round.

Once you have read and talked about some poems, encourage learners to contribute ideas to develop a class poem on the board. Then ask learners to write their own poems using a writing frame such as this one:

My friend the alien has seven blue toes,

My friend the alien has _____ nose.

Here learners need to include adjectives, not rhyming words.

Move on to frameworks where the learner completes the line with a rhyming word. For example:

My friend the alien has seven blue toes,

My friend the alien _____.

It may be necessary to ask learners to generate a list of words that rhyme with 'toes' to help them before they do this.

Ask learners to do activities 2 and 3.

Answers
1 feathers; furry; four

Workbook page 35

Sounds and spelling

Here learners complete a dot-to-dot in the shape of a fish using capital letters.

Before learners do this activity, practise the alphabet. Then give learners practice writing the capital letter that corresponds to a given lower case letter. You could write the lower case letters on the whiteboard or hold up lower case alphabet cards.

Weekly review

Use this rubric to assess learners' progress as they worked through the activities this week.

Level	Reading	Listening and speaking
■	This group know the names of most letters in the English alphabet. They can say or sing alphabet songs.	This group can learn and recite a verse of poetry. The alliterative language made fluency difficult in *A Fine Feathered Fish*.
●	This group know the names of all the letters in the English alphabet. They can recite most of the alphabet in sequence.	This group can learn and recite poetry using some expression.
▲	This group know the names of all the letters in the English alphabet. They can recite the alphabet.	This group can learn and recite poetry speaking clearly and with expression.

End of unit assessment

PCM 23 can be used to assess learners' ability to work with rhyming words. Hand a copy of the PCM to each learner and ask them to complete it independently. Collect their work, check it and record the results on a record sheet.

Unit 6 Food

Unit overview

The focus is on non-fiction texts about types of food. Learners will have the opportunity to read information about food types supported by illustrations and they will be expected to find information from illustrations, text, labels, captions and signs.

Most school curricula deal with the topic of food and healthy eating in some way. This unit will supplement any work done on this topic in health or science lessons.

This topic also allows learners to discuss and explore cultural, religious and regional aspects of food and eating. It is valuable for learners to learn that different communities eat different types of food depending on where they live, what is available locally and what beliefs and traditions they subscribe to.

Reading	Writing	Listening and speaking
1R05 Blend to read, and segment to spell, words with final and initial adjacent consonants, e.g. b–l, n–d. 1R06 Use phonic knowledge to read decodable words and to attempt to sound out some elements of unfamiliar words. 1R10 Read a range of common words on sight. 1R11 Enjoy reading and listening to a range of books, drawing on background information and vocabulary provided. 1R12 Make links to own experiences. 1R16 Read aloud independently from simple books 1R18 Identify sentences in a text. 1Rx1 Read labels, lists and captions to find information.	1W03 Know that a capital letter is used for 'I', for proper nouns and for the start of a sentence. 1W06 Develop strategies to build vocabulary. 1Wa1 Write simple storybooks with sentences to caption pictures. 1Wa2 Use relevant vocabulary. 1Wa4 Begin to use some formulaic language, e.g. Once upon a time. 1Wa6 Write simple information texts with labels, captions, lists, questions and instructions for a purpose. 1Wt1 Write a sequence of sentences retelling a familiar story or recounting an experience. 1Wp2 Compose and write a simple sentence with a capital letter and a full stop. 1Ws2 Spell familiar common words accurately, drawing on sight vocabulary. 1Ws3 Use rhyme and relate this to spelling patterns.	1SL2 Converse audibly with friends, teachers and other adults. 1SL4 Answer questions and explain further when asked. 1SL5 Speak confidently to a group to share an experience. 1SL6 Take turns in speaking. 1SL7 Listen to others and respond appropriately.

Related resources
- Slideshow 6: Food
- Audio files: *Fish and seafood*; *Fruit and vegetables*; *Dairy and eggs*; *Bread and cereals*
- Image 4: Picture of tropical fish
- PCM 24: End of unit assessment

Introducing the unit
The unit could be introduced by asking learners to talk about their favourite foods. Discuss different meal times, at what time of day different meals are eaten and what types of food are eaten at different meals. During the discussion, bring the conversation round to the different types of food that learners eat and so to the different food groups.

If possible, make a range of information about food available to the class. This can be in the form of books, articles, short videos or information from the internet. Draw up a table like this one:

Foods from plants	Foods from animals	Healthy foods	Unhealthy foods

Give learners some time to engage with the information available and then ask them to provide information to complete the table.

58

Week 1

Student's Book pages 51–53

Workbook pages 36–37

Student's Book page 51

Listening and speaking

Read the title of the unit with learners and then ask them to look at the chart on page 51. It is a pie chart but at this stage it need only be referred to as a chart. (A pie chart is a circle divided into sections.) Ask learners what they think the chart shows. Read the labels for each section of the chart with learners and ask them to point to each section in turn. Then ask questions, for example:

- Which foods should we eat most of? How can you tell from looking at the chart?

- Which food should we not each too much of? How can you tell from looking at the chart?

Ask learners to work in pairs. Give them time to look at the chart, talk about the food groups and what foods belong to each group. They should use the pictures that surround the chart and think of some other foods and where they belong.

Draw the class together and establish what the five food groups are. Write them on the whiteboard as headings and invite learners to name a food and to say which heading it should go under. Act as scribe.

Support: Help learners to read the text starting 'Food gives …' by asking questions. For example:

- What do you think it is going to be about?

- Are there any words that you know?

If necessary, ask learners to find specific words, for example: 'food', 'energy' and 'five'. When they have found 'five', ask: 'What do you think the word after "five" is?' Here learners should use the *gr* consonant cluster at the beginning of the word and the context of what they have been talking about to work out 'groups'.

Writing

Before learners turn to this section, spend some time talking about why we need food.

Learners need to use information from the text in the previous section to complete two sentences. They could then copy the first sentences onto paper and draw a picture of themselves doing something that needs energy. Under the picture they could write a caption, for example, 'I need energy to

dance/play football/run/jump.' This could be displayed with a heading such as 'Food gives us energy'.

Answer
energy; each of the five food groups

Workbook page 36

Writing

Recap the five food groups and invite learners to give one or two suggestions of foods that belong to each group. Write some of these on the whiteboard; they will help learners when they need to write themselves.

Point out the headings and ask learners to read them. Encourage learners to use initial sounds/clusters to help. Highlight the clusters *br* and *fr*; highlight *sh* where two letters make one sound; and highlight 'eggs' which has the common word ending –*s*. Learners should also note the word 'and' in each heading. Then invite them to say which food group is missing from the activity (sugar and fats).

Support: If learners need help, scribe the foods they say for the different food groups.

Student's Book page 52

Reading

Tell learners that they are going to find out more about one of the food groups – fish and seafood.

Ask learners to work in pairs. They should look at the pictures and try to identify what they can see. Then draw learners together and discuss the first two pictures. Ask questions like:

- What are the pictures of?

- Who uses fishing nets/rods?

- Where do people catch fish?

Try to elicit answers that will highlight vocabulary that is introduced in the text. Then ask learners to work in pairs and read the first paragraph about fish. Remind them to think about what they have been talking about as they read.

Read the paragraph together as a class before inviting individuals to read aloud. Then give learners time to read the rest of the text.

Remind learners again of the importance of looking at the pictures as they read – the pictures give information about what the text is about and, along with phonics and context clues, can help with reading some interest words. Follow up by asking learners what information they have learnt about fish and seafood. Then ask:

- Is a lobster a fish or a sea creature?
- Is a tuna a fish or a sea creature?
- Which is the odd one out – prawn, octopus, eel or oyster? Why?

Ask learners which part of the text has information about seafood, where fish live, different kinds of fish and about fishing. It is important that learners begin to understand the importance of interacting with the text. Spend as much time as necessary on reading and understanding the text.

Student's Book page 53

Reading and writing

In this section learners complete sentences about fish. Remind them to use the text on page 52 to find and check answers.

Answers
1 water
2 rivers;　lakes;　the sea
3 fishing rods;　nets

Listening and speaking

Ask learners to work in pairs and look at the seafood in the pictures. Can they read the seafood words? Can they describe the different types shown? Then look at the words learners are not sure about and encourage them to use clues to work them out. For example, 'octopus' and 'oyster' both start with *o*. Can any other sounds in the words help? What sound is at the end of each word?

Writing

Following on from the previous activity, learners are asked to draw three types of seafood and label them. Remind them to write the labels close to the pictures.

Listening and speaking

In this activity learners work in pairs to answers two questions. If there is time, ask them to discuss some more questions. For example:

- Do you like eating fish and seafood?
- When do you eat it?
- How is it cooked?

Learners could then give a short presentation about fish and seafood to their peers. Give them time to prepare. Monitor how clearly they speak and if they show some awareness of their audience.

Workbook page 37

Reading and writing

In this activity learners choose the correct word to match a picture of fish or seafood. They then write the words.

Monitor the activity and assess how well learners can use initial sounds as a first strategy to read the words if they are not immediately known.

Extension: Ask learners to make an underwater scene. Show them a picture of tropical fish and discuss the colours and shapes of the fish. Learners then paint or draw pictures of brightly coloured fish on paper and cut them out. To make the underwater scene, they stick their pictures on a large sheet of paper. They can refer to Student's Book pages 42–44 in Unit 5: Funny Fish before they do this.

Answers
crab; eel; octopus; prawn; squid; mackerel; lobster; mussels

Weekly review

Use this rubric to assess learners' progress as they worked through the activities this week.

Level	Reading	Listening and speaking
■	This group can use initial sounds as an initial strategy to read some interest words but then they need some support.	This group can make a short presentation to their peers but need some prompts to keep to the topic being discussed.
●	This group use initial sounds as an initial strategy and then, using the context of the word, are able to read most interest words.	This group can make a short presentation to their peers.
▲	This group use initial sounds as an initial strategy and then, using the context of the word, are able to read interest words.	This group can confidently make a short presentation to their peers.

Week 2

Student's Book pages 54–57

Workbook pages 38–39

Student's Book page 54

Listening and speaking

Tell learners that they are going to read and find out about another food group – fruit and vegetables.

1 Read the heading and the first two sentences before inviting learners to read them. Then ask learners what else they might find out about food and vegetables. Give them time to look at the pictures and read the labels, the captions and the text. Learners work in pairs to read and find out as much information as they can. Monitor what strategies learners are using and how successfully they are using them.

Support: Work with a small group to help them with the text. Guide them by asking questions. For example:

- What do you think we are going to learn about on this page?
- (pointing to a picture of, for example, a banana) What is this a picture of?
- Is a banana a fruit or a vegetable?
- Can you show me the word that says 'banana'?

Draw the class together to read the text. Start by asking learners to read the labels for the fruit. Emphasise that the label matches the picture. Discuss the different vocabulary used: 'fruit', 'trees', 'vines', 'skins', 'peeled' and 'stones'. This will help learners to use the context when reading the text.

Invite learners to read the sentences about fruit, encouraging them to use strategies – phonics, picture and label clues, and context. Then use the same strategies to help learners to read about vegetables.

Follow up by asking learners what they have found out about fruit and vegetables from the pictures and the text. They should read the relevant part of the text again if they need to clarify anything.

Spend as much time as necessary on this activity, ensuring accurate decoding and understanding of the text.

2 Learners work in pairs and answer the questions. They have the opportunity to talk about fruit and vegetables, which ones they eat and like, and which ones they have tried and not liked.

Student's Book page 55

Reading and writing

1 Using the text on page 54 as a reference, learners complete the sentences. Remind them to use the text to find and check answers.

2 Before learners do the activity, recap which fruits have large stones and which fruits have skin that needs to be peeled before it is eaten.

3–4 These activities are similar to activities 1 and 2, but with the focus on vegetables.

Learners could learn the following rhyme about chopping vegetables at this point.

Chop, chop, choppity, chop,

Cut off the bottom and cut off the top.

What we have left we will put in the pot.

Chop, chop, choppity, chop.

Extension: Make a simple pictograph or block graph to show learners' favourite fruit (or vegetable). Limit the number of fruits to six. Ask learners to choose which of the six fruits they like best and add a drawing of the fruit to the correct column of the graph. (The pieces of paper should be cut to suit the size of the graph.) Make sure they label the graph correctly and that they give it a heading to make its meaning clear. (See mathematics framework for more information on this topic if necessary.)

Answers
1 healthy foods; trees; vines; peeled; stones
3 plants; parts

Workbook page 38

Writing

Before learners do the activity, give them the opportunity to make a fruit salad.

From a selection of fruit (real or pretend) ask what you need to do first, next and so on, eliciting the words 'peel', 'chop', 'mix' and 'eat'. Carry out each part of the task commenting on what you are doing. For example: 'First I peel the mango'. The activity has four parts to the instructions – first, next, then, last of all. Elicit from learners how these words help with the order.

Put learners in groups of four. Each person in the group is responsible for one part of the instructions. Give learners time to sequence the instructions before asking each group of four to report their instructions.

Learners should then complete the instruction framework. Again some learners may benefit from you acting as scribe for this activity. This would allow you to assess if they can sequence events without getting caught up with handwriting and spelling. You could perhaps write the first two or three sentences in the sequence with them writing the rest.

Student's Book page 56

Reading

Tell learners that they are going to read and find out about another food group – dairy and eggs. Ask learners to point to the heading on page 56 and read it together. Then ask them to look at the pictures about milk. Give learners a little time to look at the pictures before asking them to describe each picture.

Discuss the pictures, highlighting words that appear in the text. Then give learners some

time to read the text in pairs. Tell them that they will be reading about what happens to milk after it comes from a cow or other animal. Remind them about the strategies they have used previously when reading text.

Follow the same procedure for the part of the text that deals with dairy products and eggs. Then ask questions to check understanding. For example:

- What animals do we get milk from?
- What do we call the truck that takes the milk from the farm to the dairy?
- What foods are made from milk?

Spend as much time as necessary on this activity to ensure accurate decoding and understanding of the text.

Student's Book page 57

Reading and writing

1 This activity requires learners to use information from the text to complete and copy sentences about milk.

2 Before learners draw a story map, refer to the relevant pictures on page 56. Discuss what is happening in each picture and write some key words on the whiteboard.

Put learners in groups of three. Each learner in a group should take one part of the sequence that describes what happens from the time the cows are milked to the time the milk is bottled. The group then tell their story to their peers. After learners tell the story correctly, ask them to draw three pictures to show what happens to milk.

3 This activity asks learners to write captions under each picture.

Support: Some learners may need support to do this. The learner says what happens and the teacher scribes what happens.

4 Learners are asked to make a list of foods that are made from milk. Remind learners how a list is written.

5 Learners are asked to use information from the text to complete sentences about eggs.

6 Before learners complete the activity, discuss with them how ice cream is made and what makes one kind of ice cream different from another – flavour. Elicit different flavours of ice cream, for example: chocolate, mint, strawberry and vanilla. (Learners may well come up with some very interesting flavours.) Learners may want to add toppings to their ice cream and they would have to include these in the ingredients.

Extension:

1 Learners could draw a picture of their new flavoured ice cream on paper. They could then cut out the picture and use it to make a display with labels and a heading.

2 Use this simple poem below as a model and ask learners to make up their own rhyming lines linking people's names with food. If they struggle, you could give them a list of foods as a starting point, for example, egg, stew, peas, macaroni, cake, papaya and melon, and ask them to think of names that rhyme with each type.

> For a project on food
>
> I asked my friends "What is good?"
>
> Betty said spaghetti,
>
> Louise said cheese,
>
> Murray said curry,
>
> Anna said banana,
>
> Ted said bread,
>
> Sam said yam,
>
> Trish said fish,
>
> Sue said callaloo,
>
> No, wait! Maybe stew.
>
> What about you?
>
> By Karen Morrison

Answers
1 milk;   cows (goats and sheep)
5 hens;   boxes;   sell

Workbook page 39

Sounds and spelling

Use the word 'egg' to highlight that some words in English end with a double consonant. Ask learners what they notice about the word 'egg' and highlight the double *gg*.

Highlight any other words with double consonants at the end that learners might know, for example: 'add', 'bell' and 'class'. Tell learners that the two letters need to be written but only one sound is made. They should learn to read and spell words ending in –*ss*, –*ff* and –*ll*. Some learners will have investigated this in Unit 3.

Remind learners that consonant-vowel-consonant (CVC) words do not end in –*s*, –*f* or –*l*, with the exceptions of 'gas', 'bus', 'has' and 'his'. (**Note:** The *s* in 'has' and 'his' sounds like *z*.) The mnemonic '**S**illy **f**oolish **l**etters, they don't stand on their own' might help learners to remember the rule.

Dictation: Use these words for dictation in this unit: 'mess', 'kiss', 'pass', 'toss', 'boss', 'less', 'miss', 'lass', 'loss', 'moss', 'hiss', 'mass'; 'doll', 'bell', 'till', 'pill', 'fell', 'bill', 'will', 'tell', 'fill', 'ill', 'sell', 'hill', 'well'; 'cuff', 'huff', 'muff', 'puff'.

The activity on Workbook page 39 asks learners to use the letters in the boxes to make new rhyming words ending in –*ff*, –*ss* and –*ll*. When they have finished the activity, invite learners to say what words they have made and highlight the double consonants.

Answers

cuff	less	pass
huff	mess	glass
puff	dress	brass
stuff	press	class

tell	hill	loss
bell	pill	toss
well	spill	moss
sell	frill	boss
smell	still	cross

Weekly review

Use this rubric to assess learners' progress as they worked through the activities this week

Level	Reading	Listening and speaking
■	This group can tell a sequence of sentences as instructions to make a fruit salad. After having the first instructions scribed, they can write the rest.	This group need some support to work as a group of three or four to tell a sequence of events.
●	This group can write a sequence of sentences as instructions to make a fruit salad with minimal support.	This group can work in threes or fours to tell a sequence of events. They need some reminding about turn taking.
▲	This group can write a sequence of sentences as instructions to make a fruit salad.	This group can work in threes or fours to tell a sequence of events, taking turns to speak.

Week 3

Student's Book pages 58–60

Workbook pages 40–41

Student's Book page 58

Reading

Tell learners that they are going to read and find out about another food group – bread and cereals.

Remind learners about the strategies they have used previously when reading text. Follow up by asking them about bread and cereals and encourage them to refer back to the pictures and text on page 58 to check the accuracy of answers.

Spend as much time as necessary on this activity to ensure accurate decoding and understanding of the text.

Student's Book page 59

Reading and writing

1 In this activity learners use information from the text to complete sentences about bread.

2 In this activity learners make a list of three different types of bread.

Answers
1 flour; wheat; fields
2 (possible answers: any three of the following) baguette, challah, croissant, naan, pitta

Listening and speaking

Elicit from learners the component parts of a sandwich, in other words, bread and a filling.

Before learners talk about making a sandwich, remind them to use words like 'first', 'next', 'then' and 'last of all'. They should then tell their peers how to make a sandwich. Learners should know that they will be asked to do this before working with their partner.

Working in pairs, learners tell each other what they like to put in a sandwich.

Extension: More able learners could report back on the discussion by writing 'How to make a sandwich' using a writing frame with the headings 'What I need' and 'What I do'.

Reading and writing

In this activity learners use information from the text on page 58 to complete sentences about rice and then copy them.

Answers
shallow water;   paddy fields

Listening and speaking

This activity gives learners the opportunity to talk in pairs about how rice is cooked and eaten in their home. This could be another opportunity for them to give a short presentation to their peers about how they eat rice at home.

Student's Book page 60

Reading and writing

This activity focuses on sugary and fatty foods. Discuss why it is important not to eat too many of them.

1 In this activity learners draw and label some sugary and fatty foods.

2 In this activity learners design a cover for a book about food. Remind them that a cover usually shows the reader what the content of the book will be about. Use non-fiction books from the class library to illustrate this and discuss what is on the cover – title, art work, author's name, illustrator's name.

3 In this activity learners write a contents page for their food book. Again, use non-fiction books to illustrate how a contents page is laid out and show one on the whiteboard.

Discuss the sections in this unit and what each section is called. Ask questions like:

- How many sections are there?
- What is the first section about?
- What is the fourth section about?
- What page number will you write beside the section about fruit and vegetables?

Workbook page 40

Reading and writing

Read the instructions with learners and make sure that they understand what they have to do. Discuss with them what signs they might include, for example, about prices, special offers and signs to encourage shoppers, for example, 'Fresh Bread', 'BREAD BAKED TODAY'. Talk about what would be a good name for the stall.

Workbook page 41

Reading

In this section learners decorate the border of a plate and draw a meal that they would like to eat. Remind them that the meal should be balanced and should include some of the foods they have learnt about.

Weekly review

Use this rubric to assess learners' progress as they worked through the activities this week.

Level	Reading	Listening and speaking
■	This group know the parts of a book and are aware that texts can look different. They can identify non-fiction books.	This group have shown improvement when presenting to their peers. They speak more clearly and are better able to keep to the topic.
●	This group know the parts of a book and are aware that texts have different purposes and look different. They can identify non-fiction books.	This group speak clearly and audibly when presenting to their peers.
▲	This group know the parts of a book and are aware that texts have different purposes and look different. They can identify non-fiction books.	This group speak clearly and audibly when presenting to their peers. They choose words carefully to express what they want to say.

End of unit assessment

Use PCM 24 to assess whether learners are able to find and record information about food groups. Hand out a copy of PCM 24 to each learner and ask learners to complete them. Tell them that they can use the information texts in the unit to find any answers that they do not know. Observe them as they work to make sure they know how to search efficiently for information using headings and the structure of the text.

Unit 7 Traditional stories

Unit overview

As learners work through this unit, they will read a story aloud and then retell and talk about the events in the story. *The Small Bun* is a story based on the traditional story *The Gingerbread Man*.

The unit could follow on from listening to other traditional stories as part of learners' experience of listening to a range of books.

Learners will further develop their appreciation of direct speech in stories.

They will have the opportunity to make simple inferences about characters.

They will have the opportunity to read and write high frequency words and other familiar words.

Reading	Writing	Listening and speaking
1R06 Use phonic knowledge to read decodable words and to attempt to sound out some elements of unfamiliar words.	1Wa1 Write simple storybooks with sentences to caption pictures.	1SL4 Answer questions and explain further when asked.
1R08 Join in with reading familiar, simple stories and poems.	1Wa2 Use relevant vocabulary.	1SL5 Speak confidently to a group to share an experience.
1R10 Read a range of common words on sight.	1Wt1 Write a sequence of sentences retelling a familiar story or recounting an experience.	1SL6 Take turns in speaking.
1R13 Retell stories, with some appropriate use of story language.	1Wp2 Compose and write a simple sentence with a capital letter and a full stop.	1SL7 Listen to others and respond appropriately.
1R16 Read aloud independently from simple books	1Ws1 Begin to learn common spellings of long vowel phonemes, e.g. 'ee', 'ai', 'oo'.	1SL8 Listen carefully to questions and instructions.
1R17 Pause at full stops when reading.	1Ws2 Spell familiar common words accurately, drawing on sight vocabulary.	
1Ri1 Anticipate what happens next in a story.	1Ws3 Use rhyme and relate this to spelling patterns.	
1Ri2 Talk about events in a story and make simple inferences about characters and events to show understanding.		

Related resources

- Slideshow 7: Traditional stories
- Audio files: *The Small Bun*; *Recipe for buns*
- Image 5: A variety of buns
- PCM 25: Phonics *ee*
- PCM 26: Phonics *oa*
- PCM 27: Phonics *ai*
- PCM 28: End of unit assessment

Introducing the unit

Remind the class that you have read many stories to them and have a discussion about the different types of stories that you have read. Encourage learners to say which ones they liked and which they did not like. They should give reasons for their choices.

Bring the discussion round to traditional stories and invite learners to share the titles of any that they know, for example: *The Six Fools, How the Zebra Got its Stripes, The Lion and the Mouse, Jack and the Beanstalk* and the Anansi tales. Tell learners that they are going to read a story based on a traditional story called *The Gingerbread Man*. Explain that folk tales are popular stories that have been passed down from one generation to the next in the spoken form, before ever being written.

There are often many versions of the story and these versions differ from place to place, and the details change from culture to culture. Discuss why this might be. Ask learners if they know of any other folk tales, and talk about any they might have read or heard.

Week 1

Student's Book pages 61–66

Workbook pages 42–43

Student's Book page 61

Reading and writing

Give learners time to look at the picture of the front cover of the book and ask them to read the instructions individually or in pairs. Then draw the class together and invite them to read aloud what they are being asked to do. Model correct reading and ensure that learners understand what is being asked of them before setting them to do the activity.

Draw learners together and talk about the discussion points as a class. Read the title of the book and ask if anyone knows what a bun is. (A bun is a small bread or bread roll. Some buns are sweet. They come in different shapes and sizes but are most commonly hand-sized or even smaller, with a round top and a flat bottom.) Show learners some pictures of buns. Then invite them to say what they think the story is going to be about.

Listening and reading

Play the audio file or read the story to learners.

Read the story again while learners follow in their books. This time, while they listen and follow the story, they need to think about the two questions in their book:

- How many animals are in the story?
- What are their names?

Ensure that learners understand the questions before reading the story again by asking them what they need to think about whilst they listen to the story.

After you have read the story, invite learners to say what they have been listening for. They may give different answers, but encourage them to refer back to the story and find evidence for their answers if they disagree.

Answers
1 three 2 sheep, goat, fox

Student's Book pages 62–65

Reading and writing

1 Spend as much time as necessary on this section to ensure correct decoding of the text and to encourage reading with fluency. Monitor and assess the needs of different learners as they use strategies – phonic skills, context and grammatical clues, reading on and rereading – to work out any unknown word.

Support: Use records and ongoing assessment to determine the next steps for individual learners who are struggling.

2–4 Ask learners to read questions 2–4 in this section and check that they know what they have to do before they complete the activities.

Answers
4 a hungry man; two; the small bun hopped off the dish and ran; possible answers include: cross, sad, worried and the learners may have their own words too

Workbook page 42

Reading and writing

Ask learners to read to page 62 in the Student's Book. Then ask: 'What did the sheep say?' Learners then work in pairs to find and read the words that the characters actually said. For example:

> page 62
>
> Sheep: "Lunch! Yummy-yum!"
> Small Bun: "I am too fast for the man and his wife, and I am too fast for you!"
>
> page 64
>
> Small Bun: "Why have you stopped?"
> Fox: "To eat you!"

Then invite pairs of learners to read aloud the words of a pair of characters. Encourage them to use different voices to suit the situation and the characters.

Now ask learners to do the activity, matching what the fox said with the picture of the fox, and what the small bun said with the picture of the small bun.

Answers
Small bun: I am too fast for the man and his wife.; If I get on your back, you will eat me!; Why have you stopped?
Fox: You have beaten me.; Trust me.; To eat you!; Get on my back and I will carry you across the river.

Student's Book page 66

Sounds and spelling

This section focuses on two letters – ee – making one sound, as in 'feet', 'peel', 'sleep' and 'sheep'.

Tell learners that they need to listen for the sound in the middle of some words. Then say words like 'feet', 'keep', 'heel' and 'weed' and ask learners what sound they hear in the middle of each word. Confirm the long vowel sound *ee* and show how it is written – *ee*. Tell learners that there are other ways to write this sound and that they will learn about them soon.

Ask learners what kind of letter *e* is and confirm that they know it is a vowel. Explain that when two vowels come together, the first one usually sounds like its name and the other is silent. They should only say one *e* (name).

Here is a good rhyme to help learners to remember this rule:

> *When two vowels together play a game*
>
> *Only the first one says its name.*

Now say a word with *ee*, for example, 'feel', and ask how many sounds learners can hear in 'feel'. Confirm that there are three sounds and invite learners to say what they are *(f-ee-l)*. Write the word 'feel' on the whiteboard.

Ask learners how to write 'peel', 'heel', 'reel', 'wheel' and 'steel' and write them in a list under 'feel'. Ask learners to read the list of words and ask what they notice about them. Confirm that they all have *ee* in the middle and they all end in *l* – they rhyme.

Repeat the above procedure for 'deep', 'keep', 'peep', 'weep', 'sheep', 'sleep', 'steep' and 'cheep'.

Here are some other words you could investigate, read and spell with the class:

> 'feet', 'need', 'leek'
>
> 'meet', 'seed', 'meek'
>
> 'sleet', 'weed', 'peek'
>
> 'sheet', 'greed', 'seek'
>
> 'sweet', 'tweed', 'week'
>
> 'feed', 'cheek'
>
> 'speed'

Before learners do activities 1–3 in this section, check that they can identify the pictures and understand what they have to do. Ask learners to read aloud to check for accurate decoding and understanding of what is being asked.

PCM 25 gives further practice of writing words with *ee*.

Dictation: Use these or similar sentences for dictation in this unit.

- We can feed the sheep.
- The bee is in the tree.
- I will go to the park next week.
- The wheel is in the shed.
- I need to meet my sister this week.
- She plants seeds and pulls out weeds.

Once learners have mastered the double *ee* sound, you could take the opportunity to ask them to identify if the vowel in the middle of words is a short *e* (sound) or a long *e* (name) in spoken words, for example: 'red', 'sleep', 'teeth', 'get', 'pet', 'sweet', 'bleed', 'pen', 'need', 'bed' and 'wheel'.

Answers
1 sheep; wheel; sweet; teeth
2 bee; tree; three
3 sheep; bee; three

Workbook page 43
Reading and writing
1 Before learners do this activity, give them practice answering questions similar to those in the activity. There is a change in tense from the question to the answer so learners should practise this orally before writing. Ask learners questions like:

- Where did you meet your Gran?
- Where did you meet your friend?

Learners should give answers like:

- I met my Gran at the shops.
- I met my friend in the park.

Learners then write the answers to the questions in activity 1. The beginning of each answer is given, but remind learners to use a full stop at the end of the sentence.

2 This activity asks learners to complete a sentence from *The Small Bun*. The words given are all high frequency words.

Ongoing opportunities should be given to practise spelling high frequency words.

Answers
1
The bun met the sheep by the gate.
The bun met the goat in the lane.
The bun met the fox by the river.
2
for; his; the; you; said

Weekly review

Use this rubric to assess learners' progress as they worked through the activities this week.

Level	Reading	Writing
■	This group can identify the words that characters speak in text with some support.	This group can spell words with the long vowel phoneme *ee* in rhyming lists and in dictated sentences most of the time.
●	This group can identify the words that characters speak in text.	This group can spell words with the long vowel phoneme *ee* in dictated sentences and in their own writing most of the time.
▲	This group can identify the words that characters speak in text.	This group can spell words with the long vowel phoneme *ee* in dictated sentences and in their own writing.

Week 2

Student's Book pages 67–68

Workbook pages 44–45

Student's Book page 67

Sounds and spelling

This section focuses on two letters – *oa* – making one sound, as in 'goat'.

1 Tell learners that they need to listen for the sound in the middle of some words. Then say words like 'coat', 'boat', 'road' and 'soap' and ask learners what sound they hear in the middle of each word. Confirm the long vowel sound *o* and show how it is written – *oa*. Tell learners that there are other ways to write this sound and that they will learn about them soon.

Ask learners what kind of letter *o* is and confirm that they know it is a vowel. Remind them that when two vowels come together, the first one usually sounds like its name and the other is silent. Repeat the rhyme:

> *When two vowels together play a game*
>
> *Only the first one says its name.*

Now say the word 'goat' and ask how many sounds learners can hear in 'goat'. Confirm that there are three sounds and invite learners to say what they are *(g-oa-t)*. Write the word 'goat' on the whiteboard.

Ask learners how to write 'coat', 'moat', 'float', 'stoat' and 'throat', and write them in a list under 'goat'. Then ask them to read the list of words and ask what they notice about the

words. Confirm that they all have *oa* in the middle and they all end in *t* – they rhyme.

Here are some other words you could investigate, read and spell with the class:

> 'coal', 'load', 'loan', 'toast'
>
> 'goal', 'road', 'moan', 'roast'
>
> 'foal', 'toad', 'boast'
>
> 'coast'

Before learners do activities 1–3 in this section, check that they can identify the pictures and understand what they have to do.

Learners should have ongoing opportunities to practise joining the letters and writing words when you dictate them.

PCM 26 gives further practice writing words with *oa*.

Dictation: Use these or similar sentences for dictation in this unit.

- The soap is in the sink.
- We had toast and milk.
- We went on a coach to the zoo.
- The toad swam in the pond.
- The oak tree is big.

Tell learners that you are going to say some words, and ask them if the vowel in the middle of each word is a short *o* (sound) or a long *o* (name).

Suggested words: 'float', 'cot', 'stoat', 'coat', 'not', 'spot', 'cloak', 'soap', 'clot', 'toad'

Once learners have done this, use the same procedure to teach two letters making one sound – *ai* as in 'mail'.

Here are some other words you could investigate, read and spell with the class:

- 'fail', 'hail', 'nail', 'jail', 'mail', 'nail', 'pail', 'rail', 'sail', 'tail', 'snail', 'trail'
- 'laid', 'pain', 'raid'
- 'gain', 'rain', 'pain', 'stain', 'train', 'grain', 'brain', 'Spain', 'chain'
- 'wait', 'waist'
- 'paint', 'faint'

PCM 27 can be used to reinforce and/or assess phonic awareness of double vowels with one sound.

Dictation: These sentences are suitable for dictation as you work through this unit.

- We will wait for the train.
- Zack got wet feet in the rain.
- The snail is on the grass.
- The dog has a long tail.
- Mum will need red paint.

Answers
1 goat; boat; coat
2 road – toad; coast – toast; goal – foal; soak – cloak
3 coat, boat, moat; loan, moan, groan; coast, roast, boast

Workbook page 44

Sounds and spelling
Before learners do this activity, give them practice in identifying the sound that they hear in the middle of words. Say some words and ask learners if the sound in the middle is *ee* or *oa*. They could point to or hold up a card or piece of paper with the letters *ee* or *oa* written on them. Alternatively, they could write *ee* or *oa* when you say a word.

Suggested words: 'road', 'keep', 'boat', 'goal', 'peep', 'steep', 'float', 'fleet', 'feet', 'roast'

In this section learners choose *ee* or *oa* to complete words and then write the words. Again, check that learners can identify the pictures before they do the activity.

Answers
goal; feet; road; peel; heel; toad; tree; goat

Student's Book page 68

Reading and writing
1 Before learners do the activity, ask them to pretend they are the sheep, the goat or the fox. Tell them to look at page 3 for the sheep, page 5 for the goat and pages 7, 10 and 12 for the fox. Then ask them to choose one animal and say the words in the way that their chosen animal might have spoken. For example:

Fox: "What a plump little bun!"

2 Learners practise writing four high frequency words that have appeared in the story. Learning to read and spell high frequency words should be an ongoing activity.

3 Learners are asked to use the high frequency words to complete and copy sentences from the story.

Answers
1 fox; sheep; goat
3 have; my; me; you

Workbook page 45

Reading and writing
This activity involves learners imagining they are the small bun and telling its story.

1 Ask learners to tell the story from the point of view of the small bun. They need to tell the story with the events in the correct order. Encourage them to use the words 'first', 'next', 'then' and 'last of all'.

The activity assesses if learners can retell the story and spell the words used. With the exception of 'table' and 'me' the words are consonant-vowel-consonant (CVC) words, or words with two letters representing one sound, as in 'dish', 'sheep', 'goat' and 'back'.

2 Learners read their story aloud and check that it makes sense.

Answers
man; dish; sheep; goat; fox; back; fox; me

Weekly review
Use this rubric to assess learners' progress as they worked through the activities this week.

Level	Reading
■	This group can spell words with the long vowel phonemes *ee* and *oa* when the words are dictated in a mixed order most of the time.
●	This group can spell words with the long vowel phonemes *ee* and *oa* when the words are dictated in a mixed order and in their own writing most of the time.
▲	This group can spell words with the long vowel phonemes *ee* and *oa* when the words are dictated in a mixed order and in their own writing.

Week 3

Student's Book pages 69–70

Workbook pages 46–47

Student's Book page 69

Reading and writing
Before learners do the activities in this section, remind them about the style of instruction texts using 'How to make a fruit salad' (see Unit 6) as an example. Discuss ingredients and instructions. Focus on the importance of the order of the instructions.

1 This activity focuses on a recipe for making buns: the ingredients needed and the method. Write the word 'ingredients' on the board and check that learners know what it means. Ask them what ingredients they might need to bake buns, for example: flour, sugar, eggs and butter. Discuss what they would do with the ingredients to make the buns, focusing on the method in the activity. Use the recipe to discuss the ingredients and the equipment needed before learners read the recipe.

2 If possible, show learners recipe books and point out the layout of ingredients and method.

Learners then use the pictures as a guide to write the instructions (method) in the correct order. The recipe can be used as a visual aid.

Support: Ask learners to tell you the sequence of instructions as shown in the pictures. Then support them with writing.

Extension: Do a simple baking activity with learners.

Answers
Mix the ingredients well.; Put the mixture into a baking tray.; Put the tray in the oven.; Take the tray out of the oven when the buns are ready.; Leave the buns to cool.

Workbook page 46

Reading
This section focuses on the feelings of the man and his wife when the bun ran away.

1 Ask learners to think about how the man and his wife might have felt when they sat down to eat the small bun, eliciting words like 'happy', 'hungry', and so on. Then ask how they might have felt when the bun ran away, eliciting words like 'cross', 'sad', 'worried', and so on. Write the words on the whiteboard.

Ask learners to do activity 1.

2 In this activity learners draw a picture of the man and his wife as the bun hopped off the dish. Discuss what facial expressions the people might have, and encourage learners to try to draw the expressions.

Extension: More able learners could add speech bubbles to the characters and write what they might have said.

Student's Book page 70

Reading and writing
1 Learners are asked to write the names of the characters in the story.

2 Before learners do the activity, ask them to think again about how the man and his wife felt when the small bun ran away and what they might have said. Then ask them to work

in pairs, taking the roles of the man and his wife, and act out the scene. Learners then write what each character might have said.

3 Learners draw a story map of the small bun's meeting with the sheep, the goat and the fox. Discuss with learners what would be in each picture. For example, there might be a gate and grass in the picture with the sheep, a lane in the picture with the goat, and a river in the picture with the fox.

4 Learners write captions under each picture.

Support: Support learners by asking them to write one, two or three captions. Again ask them to tell you what they are going to write first.

Extension: Put learners into groups. Each learner takes on the role of a character. The group then act out the story. Remind learners of some of the things they have been learning about, for example: using different voices, different facial expressions and speaking clearly.

Each group then gives a performance to the rest of their peers.

Answers
1 man, wife, small bun, sheep, goat, fox

Workbook page 47
Writing
Encourage learners to think of alternative endings to this story, for example: the bun jumped into the river and found he could swim; someone came to help him; he persuaded the fox not to eat him.

Ask learners to share their alternative endings with a partner and then invite individuals to share them with the class. Praise learners' ideas and highlight good sentence structure and use of vocabulary. Say things like: 'I really like the way you started that sentence. That made me want to hear more of your new ending. Well done.'

Learners do the activity. They draw a picture to show their alternative ending and write a sequence of sentences telling the new ending.

Support: After individuals or small groups have drawn the new ending for their story, invite them to tell you the new ending before helping them to write it.

Weekly review
Use this rubric to assess learners' progress as they worked through the activities this week.

Level	Writing
■	Using the picture they have drawn, this group can tell a sequence of sentences to tell a new ending to a story. Then with support, they write the new ending.
●	This group can write a sequence of sentences to tell a new ending to a story. They use some good vocabulary and spell most common words accurately.
▲	This group can write a sequence of sentences to tell a new ending to a story. They use relevant vocabulary and spell common words accurately.

End of unit assessment
Use PCM 28 to assess how well learners are able to form and write sentences. You may choose to observe learners as they work and to record your observations, or you could collect and mark their work, providing feedback and making notes about those who need further support in this area.

Unit 8 Feelings

Unit overview

As learners work through this unit they will read a story aloud, and then retell, talk about and sequence the events in the story. *The Lonely Penguin* is a story with a predictable structure and patterned language. Learners will also read facts from an information text (a fact file) about penguins.

They will have the opportunity to talk about both positive and negative feelings in a safe context and find ways of managing feelings.

The unit could be part of social and emotional development with a focus on what to do when you are feeling lonely or when you feel that you do not have friends.

Reading	Writing	Listening and speaking
1R06 Use phonic knowledge to read decodable words and to attempt to sound out some elements of unfamiliar words. 1R08 Join in with reading familiar, simple stories and poems. 1R10 Read a range of common words on sight. 1R13 Retell stories, with some appropriate use of story language. 1R16 Read aloud independently from simple books 1Ri1 Anticipate what happens next in a story. 1Ri2 Talk about events in a story and make simple inferences about characters and events to show understanding.	1Wa2 Use relevant vocabulary. 1Wa4 Begin to use some formulaic language, e.g. Once upon a time. 1Wt1 Write a sequence of sentences retelling a familiar story or recounting an experience. 1Wp2 Compose and write a simple sentence with a capital letter and a full stop. 1Ws1 Begin to learn common spellings of long vowel phonemes, e.g. *ee, ai, oo.* 1Ws2 Spell familiar common words accurately, drawing on sight vocabulary. 1Ws3 Use rhyme and relate this to spelling patterns. 1Ws4 Recognise common word endings, e.g. *–s, –ed* and *–ing.*	1SL1 Speak clearly and choose words carefully to express feelings and ideas when speaking of matters of immediate interest. 1SL2 Converse audibly with friends, teachers and other adults. 1SL6 Take turns in speaking. 1SL7 Listen to others and respond appropriately. 1SL4 Answer questions and explain further when asked.

Related resources

- Slideshow 8: Feelings
- Audio files: *The Lonely Penguin*; *FACT FILE: Penguins*
- PCM 29: Words ending in *–ed* and *–ing*
- PCM 30: Phonics *oo*
- Short film about penguins (teacher to source)
- PCM 31: End of unit assessment

Introducing the unit

The unit could be introduced by talking to learners about break times at school. Ask questions to get the discussion started. For example: 'What do you play? Who do you sit/play with? How do you feel during break times? Does anyone ever feel lonely?'

The Lonely Penguin fits well into a personal and social development programme, and all issues that arise from the discussion with learners must be addressed. It is very important to be sensitive to the feelings of those who do not seem to have any friends and to be aware of any teasing or unkindness that may arise during class discussions.

73

Week 1

Student's Book pages 71–76

Workbook page 48

Student's Book pages 71–74

Reading and writing

Ask learners to look at the picture of the front cover of the book and to read the questions. Draw the class together and invite individuals to read the questions in turn. Then allow learners to answer the questions before drawing them together again to check answers. Discuss activity 4, ensuring that learners know why this is likely to be a fiction book – the title and the art work indicate this. Ask learners what the cover might look like if it was a non-fiction book.

Extension: Petr Horáček is an award-winning author and illustrator. Learners may enjoy reading about him and his work and doing presentations on his books and his style. His own website, www.petrhoracek.co.uk, contains links to his books as well as DVDs that learners can watch. There is also a list of his awards, a biography and a blog that he updates regularly.

Answers
The Lonely Penguin;   Petr Horáček;
Petr Horáček;   fiction

Listening and speaking

1 Learners work in pairs to discuss why the penguin might be lonely. Then draw them together as a class so they can tell each other what they think the reason is.

Note: Be sensitive to the fact that answers could reflect how a learner may be feeling.

2 Before asking learners to read the story, go through it with them, asking them to describe what is happening in each picture. Highlight any vocabulary that comes from looking at the pictures and that appears in the text and write it on the whiteboard, for example: 'lonely', 'penguin', 'friends', 'snow', 'frost', 'ice', 'running', 'sliding', 'climbs', 'cold water' and 'swimming'. This will familiarise learners with the vocabulary and what happens in the story before they read.

Give learners time to read the story. Monitor how they are using phonics, and picture and context clues to work out any unknown words.

Support: It may be necessary to work with individuals to help them use strategies to read the text. Alternatively, put learners in groups

and have them listen to the audio file as they follow the story.

Draw learners together and invite individuals to read aloud while the others follow.

Spend as much time as necessary on this activity to ensure correct decoding of the text and to encourage reading with fluency. Encourage learners to use a variety of strategies – phonic skills, picture, context and grammatical clues, reading on and rereading – to work out any unknown words.

3 After reading the story, learners are asked to talk about why the penguin was lonely. Was it what they thought before they read the story? Encourage them to articulate their reasons.

Student's Book page 75

Reading and writing

Discuss with learners the different things that the lonely penguin *did* when he was looking for his friends. Encourage learners to answer in sentences. **Note:** In *The Lonely Penguin,* the story is told using the present tense, whereas learners are asked to say what the penguin *did*. In other words, they have to use a past tense. For example:

- Penguin ran through the snow.
- He slid on the frosty ice.
- He climbed up the hill.

In the activity learners look at the pictures and say what the penguin *is doing*. For example: 'Penguin *is looking* for his friends.'

Learners then read all the sentences and write the one that matches each picture.

Answers
Penguin is looking for his friends.; Penguin is running through the snow.; Penguin is sliding on the frosty ice.; Penguin climbs up the hill.; Penguin finds his friends swimming in the cold water.

Student's Book page 76

Reading and writing

This section focuses on the suffix *–ing.*

1 This activity asks learners to find words ending in *–ing* in the story *The Lonely Penguin.* Model how to do this in a systematic way. Ask learners to turn to page 1 of the text and point to any word ending in *–ing.* Show on the whiteboard how learners should write the page number and the word they find: 'Page 1 coming'. Ask learners to check if there are any words ending in *–ing* on page 2. Turn to page 3 and repeat the procedure. Then show learners how to write 'Page 3' under 'Page 1' and write the word 'looking' alongside, forming a list.

Learners do the activity. Monitor how they tackle it and assist any learners who seem to be struggling or disorganised. Observe whether:

- able readers can scan the text to find the words
- some readers need to read every word on the page before identifying the –ing word
- some learners do a bit of both.

2 Before learners do the activity, give them an opportunity to add –ing to words. At this stage, use only words whose root does not change when –ing is added. Write the root word and then add –ing to make the new word on the whiteboard. For example:

'lift' + –ing = 'lifting'
'send' + –ing = 'sending'
'crush' + –ing = 'crushing'

3 Asks learners to use the –ing words in the box to complete sentences from the text.

Answers
1 Page 1 coming; Page 3 looking; Page 5 running; Page 6 sliding; Page 7 looking; Page 11 swimming
2 looking; fishing; keeping; cooking; crashing; peeping; hooking; brushing; sleeping
3 sliding; swimming; running

Workbook page 48

Reading
This activity assesses learners' reading of familiar text in a different setting from the story in the Student's Book.

Learners are asked to circle the words ending in –ing and then to draw lines to match the beginning of each sentence with its ending. Read the instructions with learners to check that they know what they have to do and that they realise there are two parts to the activity.

Extension: Investigate the word ending –ed. Do this orally and ask learners to change from the present tense to the past tense and vice versa. For example:

- Today I am painting. Yesterday I painted.
- Yesterday I jumped. Today I am _____.
- Today it is raining. Yesterday it _____.
- What are you doing today? (A learner replies) I am washing the car.
- What did you do yesterday? (A learner replies) I walked to the shops. I washed my hair.

Use PCM 29 to reinforce and assess work on different word endings. Learners can complete this either as class activity or you can set it as homework.

Answers
Penguin is climbing up the hill.; Penguin is looking for his friends.; Penguin is running through the snow.; Penguin is sliding on the frosty ice.; Penguin is swimming in the cold water.; Penguin is jumping into the air.

Weekly review
Use this rubric to assess learners' progress as they worked through the activities this week.

Level	Writing
■	This group recognise the common word ending –ing.
●	This group recognise the common word ending –ing. They can spell most words ending in –ing where –ing is added to the root word.
▲	This group recognise the common word ending –ing. They can spell words ending in –ing where –ing is added to the root word.

Week 2

Student's Book pages 77–78

Workbook pages 49–51

Student's Book page 77

Sounds and spelling

This section focuses on two letters making one sound – *oo*, as in 'moon'.

Tell learners that they need to listen for the sound in the middle of some words. Then say words like 'room', 'cool', 'spoon' and 'broom' and ask learners what sound they hear in the middle of each word. Confirm the long vowel sound *oo* and show how it is written –*oo*. Tell learners that there are other ways to write this sound and that they will learn about them soon.

Now say the word 'cool' and ask how many sounds learners can hear in 'cool'. Confirm that there are three sounds and invite learners to say what they are (*c-oo-l*). Write the word 'cool' on the whiteboard.

Ask learners how to write 'pool', 'fool' and 'stool' and write them in a list under 'cool'. Ask learners to read the list of words and ask what they notice about them. Confirm that they all have *oo* in the middle and they all end in *l* – they rhyme.

Here are some other words you could investigate, read and spell with the class:

- 'moon', 'soon', 'noon', 'spoon'
- 'toot', 'hoot', 'root', 'shoot'
- 'room', 'zoom', 'broom', 'bloom', 'groom', 'gloom'

Before learners do the activities, ensure that they can read the instructions and that they know what they have to do.

PCM 30 gives further practice in writing words with *oo*.

Dictation: Use these or similar sentences for dictation to reinforce the spellings taught in this and previous units. The sentences include words with *ee* in the middle.

- Mum has a big spoon.
- Nick is on the stool.
- I will go to the zoo next week.
- Lee took the wheel to the shed.
- We get wool from sheep.
- Adeel will meet us soon.
- The crab is in the deep pool.

Answers

2 moon; spoon; stool
3 hoop, loop, stoop; cool, tool, stool, pool; room, zoom, broom

Workbook page 49

Sounds and spelling

Before learners do this activity, give them practice in identifying the sound that they hear in the middle of words. Say some words and ask learners if the sound in the middle is *ee* or *oo*. They could point to or hold up a card or piece of paper with the letters *ee* or *oo* written on them. Alternatively, they could write *ee* or *oo* when you say a word.

Suggested words: 'cool', 'keep', 'room', 'moon', 'sheep', 'sleep', 'broom', 'sheet', 'week', 'spoon'

In this section learners write words with *oo* or *ee* in the middle. Check that learners can identify the pictures before they do the activity.

Answers

boot; feet; week; hoop; wheel; spoon; stool; sleep

Workbook page 50

Sounds and spelling

In Unit 7 learners learned about *oa* representing the long vowel sound *o* in the middle of words. This section focuses on the vowel sound represented by *ow* at the end of words.

Tell learners that they need to listen for the sound at the end of some words. Say words like 'snow', 'blow', 'show' and 'grow' and ask learners what sound they hear at the end of each word. Confirm the long vowel sound *o* and show how it is written – *ow* – when it is at the end of a word.

Note: *ow* is the usual representation of the long vowel sound *o* when it is at the end of a single-syllable word. The exception is *oe,* as in 'toe', 'foe', 'doe', 'hoe', 'woe' and 'roe'.

Now say the word 'bow' and ask how many sounds learners can hear. Confirm that there are two sounds and invite learners to say what they are (*b-ow*). Write the word 'bow' on the whiteboard.

Ask learners how to write 'mow', 'row', 'sow' and 'tow' and write them in a list under 'bow'. Ask learners to read the list of words and say what they notice about them. Confirm that they all have *ow* at the end – they rhyme.

Repeat the procedure for 'snow', 'blow', 'crow', 'flow', 'grow' and 'show'. Draw learners' attention to the consonant clusters at the beginning of 'blow', 'crow', 'flow' and 'grow' and the two letters making one sound at the beginning of 'show'.

Learners now do the activity on Workbook page 50. Check that they can read the instructions and understand what is being asked of them.

Dictation: Use these or similar sentences for dictation to reinforce the spelling taught in this and previous units.

- The snow is deep.
- A crow is black.
- The seeds will grow in pots.
- The stool is low.
- The wind will blow the flag.
- The clock is slow.

To build on this work, ask learners if they know what are the two different ways of making the long vowel sound *o*, and confirm *oa* and *ow*. If the long vowel sound *o* is in the middle of words, how is it usually written? Confirm *oa*. This applies to single-syllable words. (Exceptions are 'own', 'bowl' and 'grown'.) If the long vowel sound *o* is at the end of words, it is usually written *ow*. (Exceptions are 'toe', 'foe', 'hoe' and 'Joe'.)

Give learners the opportunity to identify the correct representation of the long vowel sound *o* in words. They could point to or hold up a card or piece of paper with letters *ow* or *oa* written on them. Alternatively, they could write *ow* or *oa* when you say a word.

Suggested words: 'coat', 'low', 'goal', 'loaf', 'blow', 'snow', 'boast', 'grow', 'moat', 'crow', 'toast', 'cloak', 'goal', 'float', 'show', 'flow', 'boat', 'row', 'coal', 'bow', 'goat', 'road', 'moan', 'tow', 'cloak', 'soap'

Answers
2 grow; slow; blow; glow; flow; throw
3 window; rainbow; pillow

Student's Book page 78
Listening and speaking
1 Before learners do the activity, give them the opportunity to work in pairs and retell the story. Then draw the class together to recap the sequence of events in the story:

- Penguin looking for his friends
- Penguin running through the snow
- Penguin sliding on the frosty ice
- Penguin climbing up the hill
- Penguin jumping into the air
- Penguin finding his friends.

Reading and writing
In this section learners are asked to draw a story map to show the sequence of events of the penguin looking for and finding his friends. They are then asked to write captions for the pictures.

You could organise learners into groups of three for this activity, with each learner in a group taking responsibility for one picture. The pictures could be mounted in sequence for display. Learners could then discuss the captions before writing them.

Workbook page 51
Reading and writing
This section involves learners imagining that they are the penguin telling his story by completing sentences that are in sequence.

Remind learners to read what they have written and check that it makes sense. Alternatively, they can read and check a partner's work.

Support: You may need to provide the words for some learners to use.

Answers
my friends; snow; frosty ice; everywhere; the hill; the air; my friends

Weekly review

Use this rubric to assess learners' progress as they worked through the activities this week.

Level	Reading	Writing
■	This group use phonic knowledge to read decodable words, including sounds represented by more than one letter, like *sh, ch* and *ck*.	This group can spell words with long vowel phonemes when they are dictated in lists with a pattern.
●	This group use phonic knowledge, including long vowel phonemes to read decodable words.	This group can spell words with long vowel phonemes in dictation sentences and in their own writing most of the time.
▲	This group use phonic knowledge, including long vowel phonemes, to read decodable words and to attempt to sound out elements of unfamiliar words.	This group can spell words with long vowel phonemes in dictation sentences and in their own writing.

Week 3

Student's Book pages 79–80

Workbook pages 52–53

Workbook page 52

Listening and speaking

1–2 Give learners time to talk before drawing them together for a class discussion about how the penguin might have felt when he found his friends. Then discuss what makes learners happy. Highlight some vocabulary that could be used in the next section and write it on the whiteboard.

Writing

The learners write six things around the happy face that make them feel happy.

Workbook page 53

Writing

Ask learners to discuss how they could help anyone in school who might be feeling lonely. One suggestion could be to make a poster. Discuss what would be on the poster and how it would need to look to attract attention. It would be helpful to show a selection of posters to learners to illustrate features such as clear presentation, bold uncluttered pictures, style, and colour and size of print.

Student's Book page 79

Reading and speaking

Discuss with learners how the penguin in the story *The Lonely Penguin* is a character in a story. Then tell them that they are going to watch a short film and read about real penguins. There are a number of documentary films about penguins on the internet. National Geographic has some good suitable videos

(see https://www.youtube.com/watch?v=wr4d2FfivA4), as do the BBC and other broadcasters. Choose one that is suitable for your class and watch it before you show the class to make sure nothing inappropriate is included.

Encourage learners to jot down notes as they watch to remind them of any interesting or surprising facts. After watching the film, discuss the key points and ask questions to check what information learners have found out from watching it.

Tell learners that they are going to work in pairs and read a fact file about penguins. Tell them that after they have read the fact file, they should be able to tell the class two facts (one fact each) about penguins. Encourage learners to look at the photographs to get as much information from them before they read the text. Remind learners to look back at the photographs if they are having difficulty with a word. This, along with other strategies, can help them.

Support: Peer support, where a more able reader works with a less able reader, would be a good strategy to use here. Make sure that both readers become involved in the reading.

Student's Book page 80

Reading and writing

1 Learners work individually or in pairs. Ask them to read the fact file on page 79 again.

2–3 Ask learners to read the questions and make sure they understand what is being asked of them. Remind them to check their answers in the text. In activity 2, if a sentence is true, they should be able to show the evidence for their answer in the fact file.

Say two statements about penguins or write the statements on the board. (There must be evidence for the statements in the fact file.) For example:

- Penguins eat fish. (true – fourth sentence in the fact file on page 79)
- Small penguins live in colder climates. (false – seventh sentence in the fact file on page 79)

Ask learners if the first statement is true. Then ask learners to find evidence for their answer in the text. Do the same for the second statement.

Ask learners to do activities 2 and 3. Monitor how well learners do them. Do they refer back to the fact file to check answers and spelling?

Support: Support individuals as necessary with this activity. Peer support may be a good strategy for some learners.

Answers
2 Penguins are birds.; Penguins can swim.; The smallest penguin is a Little Blue.
3 fish and other small sea creatures; wings; seawater; Emperor Penguin; chick

Weekly review

Use this rubric to assess learners' progress as they worked through the activities this week.

Level	Listening and speaking
■	This group speak well, taking turns to speak in pairs or in a small group situation.
●	This group speak clearly, taking turns to speak, in pairs or in a larger group, or in a class situation. They show some awareness of the listener.
▲	This group speak clearly, taking turns to speak, in pairs or in a larger group, or in a class situation. They show awareness of the listener.

End of unit assessment

Use PCM 31 to assess phonic awareness and spelling skills. Hand out copies of the sheet and give learners time to complete it under test conditions. Display the answers and have learners check and correct each other's work. They should write a score on the sheet before returning it.

Unit 9 Catching the Moon

Unit overview

As learners work through this unit, they will read a story aloud and then retell and talk about the events in the story. *Catching the Moon* is a traditional story using a familiar context. It deals with silly ideas and looks at how people behave in family settings.

The unit could be linked to personal and social development or planning for a school event.

Learners will further develop their appreciation of direct speech in stories.

They will have the opportunity to make simple inferences about characters and their behaviour.

Reading	Writing	Listening and speaking
1R03 Identify separate sounds (phonemes) within words, which may be represented by more than one letter, e.g. *th, ch, sh*.	1W03 Know that a capital letter is used for 'I', for proper nouns and for the start of a sentence.	1SL3 Show some awareness of the listener through non-verbal communication.
1R06 Use phonic knowledge to read decodable words and to attempt to sound out some elements of unfamiliar words.	1W04 Use knowledge of sounds to write simple regular words, and to attempt other words including when writing simple sentences dictated by the teacher from memory.	1SL4 Answer questions and explain further when asked.

1SL6 Take turns in speaking. |
1R10 Read a range of common words on sight.	1Wa2 Use relevant vocabulary.	1SL7 Listen to others and respond appropriately.
1R11 Enjoy reading and listening to a range of books, drawing on background information and vocabulary provided.	1Wa3 Record answers to questions, e.g. as lists, charts.	1SL9 Engage in imaginative play, enacting simple characters or situations.
1R12 Make links to own experiences.	1Wa6 Write simple information texts with labels, captions, lists, questions and instructions for a purpose.	1SL10 Note that people speak in different ways for different purposes and meanings.
1R13 Retell stories, with some appropriate use of story language.	1Wp2 Compose and write a simple sentence with a capital letter and a full stop.	
1R16 Read aloud independently from simple books	1Ws3 Use rhyme and relate this to spelling patterns.	
1R17 Pause at full stops when reading.		
1Ri2 Talk about events in a story and make simple inferences about characters and events to show understanding.		
1Rw2 Recognise story elements, e.g. beginning, middle and end.		

Related resources

- Slideshow 9: Catching the Moon
- Audio file: *Catching the Moon*
- Image 6: Large picture of the moon
- PCM 32: Phonics *ie*
- PCM 33: End of unit assessment

80

Introducing the unit

Remind learners that they have already read a story about the moon. Ask them to look through *Bot on the Moon* again, on pages 32–34 of the Student's Book, and to recap what happened in that story. Talk about whether it is realistic to visit the moon or not.

Show learners a picture of the moon, and ask them to describe what they can see using vocabulary that they already know. Ask them whether the moon is large or small and how they know this. Point out that the moon is very large, but that it looks small because it is so far away.

Put learners in small groups. Tell them to imagine that they are a group of scientists who have been asked to try to capture the moon so that it can be studied more closely. Ask them to discuss what they would need to do and let them sketch their ideas for doing this on a large sheet of paper. When they have finished, they can share their ideas with the class. Note that the popular film *Despicable Me* deals with this idea. In this film, the characters shrink the moon and remove it from the sky. Learners can use this idea if they have seen the film.

Week 1

Student's Book pages 81–86

Workbook pages 54–55

Workbook page 54

Reading

1 Before learners read the book, ask them to look at the cover and think about what the book is going to be about. Ask them to read the instructions of activity 1 before they circle the words that they think might describe what the book will be about. Remind learners that it is important to read all the words first and that they need to circle more than one word.

Draw the class together and invite them to say which words they circled. Follow up by asking questions, for example: 'What makes you think that word tells you what the book might be about?' Such questions encourage learners to use the picture to make sensible suggestions and not just choose words randomly.

2–3 Give learners time to read the questions. Monitor for accuracy and understanding and model reading of the questions before learners do the activities.

When learners have completed the activity, draw the class together to discuss and clarify answers.

Answers
2 We can see the moon at night.
3 This is a fiction book.

Student's Book pages 81–83

Reading and listening
Play the audio file or read the story to learners. Then tell learners that you are going to read it again. This time they need to listen for the answers to the following questions:

- How many characters are in the story?
- What are the names of the characters?

Check that learners found the answers to the questions through listening.

Ask learners to read the story in pairs or individually. They then read it aloud to you. You can ask different learners to read parts of the story whilst the others follow.

Spend as much time as necessary on this section to ensure correct decoding of the text and to encourage reading with fluency. Encourage learners to use a variety of strategies, for example, phonic skills, picture and context clues, reading on and rereading, to work out any unknown words.

Ask questions to check understanding. For example:

- Hal had a tantrum. What is a tantrum?
- Why did Hal have a tantrum?
- Who went to get the moon for Hal?
- Where did the servants go to catch the moon?
- Who made the plans?
- What were the plans?

Then ask learners:

- Do you think Hal wanted the real moon? What makes you think that?
- Could it have been his toy moon? What makes you think that? (See the picture on page 1.)
- Why might Hal's parents have thought that Hal wanted the real moon?

Student's Book page 84

Reading and writing

1 Before learners read pages 1–2 of *Catching the Moon,* talk about the characters and their relationship to each other – mother, father and son.

2–3 Invite learners to read the instructions of activities 2 and 3 aloud and check that they all understand what is being asked. Learners then do the task.

Extension: Learners could write the names of the people they live with and what their relationship is to them, for example: mother, father, brother, sister, aunt, uncle, cousin, grandmother and grandfather. Remind learners to use a capital letter at the beginning of each name.

Answers
1 Hal, Queen, King
2 mother; father; son
3 He stamped his feet.; He shouted and yelled.

Workbook page 55

Reading and writing

In this section learners are asked to think about and write the names of characters from previous units.

Before learners do the activities, ask them to tell you the names of characters in books from other units, for example: Max, Bot, Grandad, Penguin, Small Bun, Bee, Fox, Goat and Sheep. Then give learners the opportunity to say the names of characters from other stories they know.

Answers
2 Grandad; Max; Bot; Small Bun; Penguin; Bee

Student's Book page 85

Reading and writing

1 Give learners time to read pages 3–4 again and then to talk about how they think the servants felt after the King said, "You must go and catch the moon."

Then draw the class together and ask:
- How might the servants have felt?
- Should the King have asked them to do that?
- Were the servants always being asked to do impossible things?

- Should the King have tried to get the moon himself?
- Should the King and Queen have said to Hal, "No, you can't have the moon"?

2 This activity asks learners to describe characters. Before learners do the activity, describe one of the people in the class and ask the class to guess which person you are describing. For example:

- This person is tall, with straight hair. (Learners who think they fit into this category can stand up.)
- This person's hair is black. (Learners whose hair is not black sit down.)
- This person wears glasses. (Learners who do not wear glasses sit down.)
- This person is wearing … (and so on, until only one person is left standing).

Repeat to describe another learner.

Then ask learners to read the words in the box and the questions. Check if there are any words that they cannot read and that they understand what to do. Learners then do the activity.

Extension: Learners could work in pairs and draw a portrait of each other. They then write a caption that describes their partner. For example:

- … has short, curly hair.
- … wears glasses.

More able learners could write fuller descriptions. The portraits and captions could be displayed with a suitable heading.

Answers
2 Grim: white hair; tall; long nose; thin; big feet
Crumb: black hair; fat nose; short; bald; glasses; fat; small feet

Student's Book page 86

Sounds and spelling

This section focuses on the long vowel *i* represented by *y*.

Tell learners that they need to listen for the sound at the end of some words. Then say words like 'my', 'by', 'shy' and 'cry' and ask learners what sound they hear at the end of each word. Confirm the long vowel sound *i*.

Ask learners which letters they have already learnt about making the long vowel sound *i* and confirm *igh*. Explain that there is another way to write this sound: *y*. Tell learners that if the long vowel sound *i* is in the middle of a word, it is usually represented by *igh,* but if it is at the end of the word, it is represented by *y*. Exceptions are 'dic', 'lie', 'pie', 'tie' and 'vie'.

Tell learners you want to write the word 'my' and ask how many sounds they can hear in the word. Confirm that there are two sounds and invite learners to say what they are (*m-y*). Write the word 'my' on the whiteboard, saying: 'The first sound is *m* and this is how we write it. The second sound is *i* and this is how we write it when it is at the end of a word: *y*. The word is "my".'

Ask learners how to write 'by', 'cry', 'dry', 'fry' and 'try'. Remember to draw their attention to the consonant clusters in 'cry', 'dry', 'fry' and 'try'.

Repeat the above procedure for 'fly', 'sly', 'sky', 'sty', 'spy', 'shy' and 'why'.

Give learners practice in identifying the correct representation of the long vowel sound *i*. Say some words and ask learners if the *i* sound is represented by *igh* or *y*. They should point

to/hold up a card or piece of paper with the letters representing the sounds *igh* and *y* written on them. Alternatively, they could write *igh* or *y* when you say a word.

Suggested words: 'night', 'shy', 'cry', 'tight', 'bright', 'light', 'why', 'by', 'flight', 'fly', 'fright', 'my', 'try', 'might', 'right', 'sky'.

Ask learners to read the instructions of the activities. Check that learners can read them and understand what is being asked of them before they do the activities.

Dictation: Use these or similar sentences as dictation to reinforce and assess the spelling rules taught in this unit.

* There is a fly on the cake.
* My mum went to see my gran.
* We will fry the fish for tea.
* Why did you cry?
* The class will try to sing the song.

Answers
2 my; cry; by; dry; try; fly; sty; spy; why; shy

Weekly review
Use this rubric to assess learners' progress as they worked through the activities this week.

Level	Reading	Writing
■	This group can read familiar text aloud and take some notice of full stops when reading.	This group can write dictated words with the long vowel sound *i* represented by *y* and *igh*.
●	This group can read aloud, pausing at full stops when reading.	This group can write dictated words and sentences with the long vowel sound *i* represented in two different ways: *y* and *igh*.
▲	This group can read aloud independently, pausing at full stops when reading.	This group can write dictated words and sentences with the long vowel sound *i* represented in three different ways. They can spell the words accurately in their own writing most of the time.

Week 2
Student's Book pages 87–88

Workbook pages 56–57

Student's Book page 87
Listening and speaking
Give learners time to talk in pairs about Crumb's plans, and then Grim and Crumb's

second plan. Then draw them together as a class to discuss why the plans didn't work.

Reading and writing
Learners are asked to make a list of things that Crumb needed for his plan. Remind learners how a list is written and that they can refer to the text to check spelling if necessary.

Support: It may be necessary to help some learners to find the page (6) where they will find the things that Crumb needed for the plan.

Answers
a ladder, a net, a big hook, some string

Sounds and spelling
This activity introduces another representation of the long vowel sound *i* – *ie*.

There are only a few single-syllable words in this category: 'die', 'lie', 'pie', 'tie' and 'vie'. It is worth encouraging learners to try to remember these words (although 'vie' is possibly not a word that learners come across in everyday situations at the moment).

Check that learners know what to do in this section and ask them to complete the activities.

PCM 32 gives further practice writing words with *ie*.

Answers
1 my; tie
2 die; pie

Workbook page 56

Reading
Write the sentence 'They set off to catch the moon.' on the whiteboard and ask a learner to read it. Write the word 'catch' on the whiteboard. Now ask learners to write the word 'match' on paper or small whiteboards. Check that they understand that they only have to change the first letter, that is, if they can spell 'catch' they can use onset and rime to spell 'match'. Then ask them to write 'batch', 'hatch', 'latch', 'patch' and 'thatch'. Ask learners to read the words they have written.

Answers
Hal wanted the moon.; You must go and catch the moon.; They set off to catch the moon.; The servants went out into the garden.; The servants put the ladder by the tree.; The servants went up to the top of the tower.; Crumb and Grim fell into the pond.

Workbook page 57

Sounds and spelling
Before learners do the activity, ask them to write the different ways that the long vowel sound *i* can be written as *igh, y* or *ie*. Then ask them to write words that you dictate with the different representations, for example: 'night', 'tie', 'my', 'shy', 'light' and 'pie'.

Extension: Here are some other words more able learners could investigate, read and spell: 'ditch', 'hitch', 'pitch', 'witch', 'stitch' and 'fetch'.

Dictation: Use these or similar sentences for dictation to reinforce and/or assess spelling rules developed in this unit.

*   Last night we saw the moon in the sky.
*   I lost my tie.
*   I might cry if I slip.
*   Why did you fight with him?

Answers
2 match – patch; fly – sky; pie – tie

Student's Book page 88

Reading and writing
This section focuses on how the characters felt and how Crumb and Grim felt at the end of the story.

1 Give learners time to talk about the discussion points in activity 1. Then draw the class together and invite learners to give their opinions about how the characters might have felt. Try to elicit some of the words in the box in activity 2. Ask:

*   Do you think the characters were right to feel the way they did?
*   How might you have felt if you were a servant?

2 In this activity learners are asked to choose and write the words that they think describe how Grim and Crumb felt.

3 Before learners do the activity, ask them to work in pairs. One person imagines they are Crumb and the other imagines they are Grim. They then speak the words their character might have said when he saw Hal sleeping in bed.

Draw the class together and invite a pair of learners to say what they think Crumb and Grim might have said and demonstrate how the words should be written in speech bubbles.

Weekly review

Use this rubric to assess learners' progress as they worked through the activities this week.

Level	Writing
■	This group can use rhyme and relate it to spelling patterns. They spell most words with regular spelling patterns accurately.
●	This group have a good understanding of rhyme and how to relate it to spelling patterns. They spell most common words accurately.
▲	This group have a very good understanding of rhyme and how to relate it to spelling patterns. They spell most common words accurately.

Week 3

Student's Book pages 89–90

Workbook pages 58–59

Workbook page 58

Reading and writing

This activity asks learners to find out who said certain words. Page references are given for learners to check their answers. Demonstrate the first one:

- Ask learners to read the first sentence.
- Ask learners what page they should turn to. (page 6)
- Ask learners to turn to page 6, read the text and find who said, "I have a plan."

Learners may know the correct answers from memory but they should be reminded to check answers in the text.

Answers
Crumb; Grim; Crumb; Hal; the King; Crumb; the King and the Queen; Grim

Student's Book page 89

Listening and speaking

Using the pictures, learners in pairs retell the story and act out the parts of Crumb and Grim while they make and carry out their plans. Discuss with learners what kind of voices the characters might have used when they were making and trying to carry out their plans.

Would their voices have remained the same throughout the activity?

Student's Book page 90

Talking and listening

This activity asks learners to think about Hal at the beginning of the story and at the end of the story. Give learners time read the questions and to talk and share their ideas. Then invite them to share their opinions about Hal. How did he change, and why? Which moon do they think Hal really wanted?

Workbook page 59

Writing

1 In this activity learners are asked to write the capital letter for the corresponding lower case letter of the alphabet.

2 Learners write the names of characters from different units correctly, that is, using a capital letter at the beginning of each name.

Talk with learners about when capital letters are always used: at the beginning of sentences and names. Talk about other uses of capital letters – in headings, titles and for emphasis. For example:

- SPLASH! page 10 of The *Lonely Penguin*

Extension: Ask learners to write the title of the book (*Catching the Moon*) in capital letters. They can decorate their title and colour the letters.

85

Weekly review

Use this rubric to assess learners' progress as they worked through the activities this week.

Level	Reading	Listening and speaking
■	This group can write a sequence of captions to tell a story with some support.	This group speak well in a group, taking turns to speak. They need some support to answer questions.
●	This group can write a sequence of captions to tell a story.	This group speak well in a group. They can answer questions and, with some support, develop their answers.
▲	This group can write a sequence of captions to tell a story. Writing is legible and punctuation and spelling is accurate.	This group speak confidently in a group and can answer questions, explaining further when asked.

End of unit assessment

Use PCM 33 to assess how well learners are able to complete sentences and say what happened next in a story. Once learners have completed the work, ask them to share their answers with the class and let them assess their own work. Ask them to write a comment on their work at the end of the activity.

86

Phonics 1

Read the words. Write the correct word for each picture.

hat cat bat	
	_____

bed red fed	
	_____

tin fin pin	
	_____

but hut nut	
	_____

Phonics 2

Read the words. Write the correct word for each picture.

bad bag bat	
bet beg bed	
hop top mop	
wig dig fig	

Phonics 3

Read the words. Write the correct word for each picture.

hut hat hit	
	_____
pet pat pot	
	_____
bid bed bud	
	_____
fix fox fax	
	_____

Phonics 4

Write the correct word for each picture.

_____

_____

_____

_____

_____

_____

Phonics 5

Write the correct word for each picture.

Phonics 6

Read the sentences.
Write the sentence that matches each picture.

	A man is in the van. A man is in the bus. _____
	The cat is on the bin. The cat is in the bin _____
	Gran can fix the tap. Gran can fix the tag. _____

Phonics 7

Write the word for each picture in the correct rhyming list.

fat   lap
sat   sap

_____   _____

_____   _____

man   jag
ran   wag

_____   _____

_____   _____

Phonics 8

Write the word for each picture in the correct rhyming list.

<table>
<tr><td>top</td><td>den</td></tr>
<tr><td>pop</td><td>men</td></tr>
</table>

top

pop

_____

_____

den

men

_____

_____

fog

dog

_____

_____

met

wet

_____

_____

✓

End of unit assessment

Read the instructions below.

❶ Cut along the dotted lines.

❷ Put the sentences in the correct order.

❸ Read and check that the story makes sense.

❹ Stick the sentences in the correct order onto paper.

❺ Read and check.

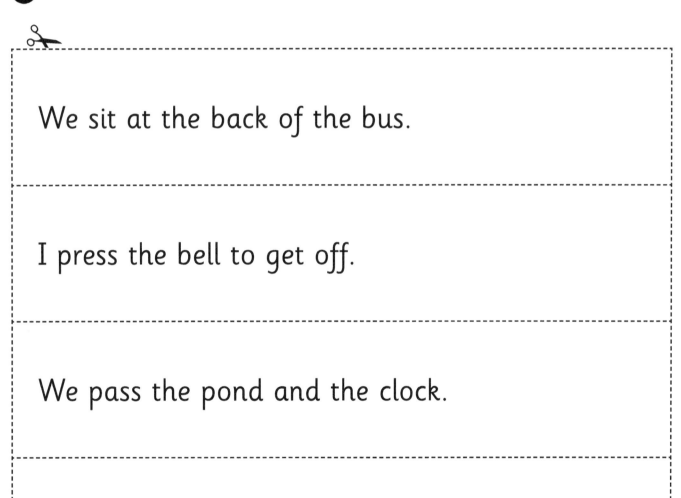

We sit at the back of the bus.

I press the bell to get off.

We pass the pond and the clock.

We get on the bus.

Words ending in –*ing*

Use the words in the box to complete the sentences.
Copy the sentences.

cooking   jumping   kicking   lifting   reading

	He is _____ _____
	He is _____ _____
	They are _____ _____
	He is _____ _____
	They are _____ _____

Phonics –sh

Complete the words. Write the words.

fi____

_____

____ell

_____

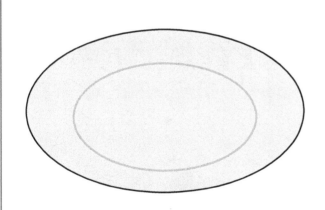

di____

_____

____elf

_____

Phonics *sh, ch, th, wh*

Colour the pictures.

- *sh* words red
- *th* words blue
- *ch* words green
- *wh* words yellow

Phonics *sh, ch, th, wh*

Write the first two letters for each picture.

| sh | ch | th | wh |

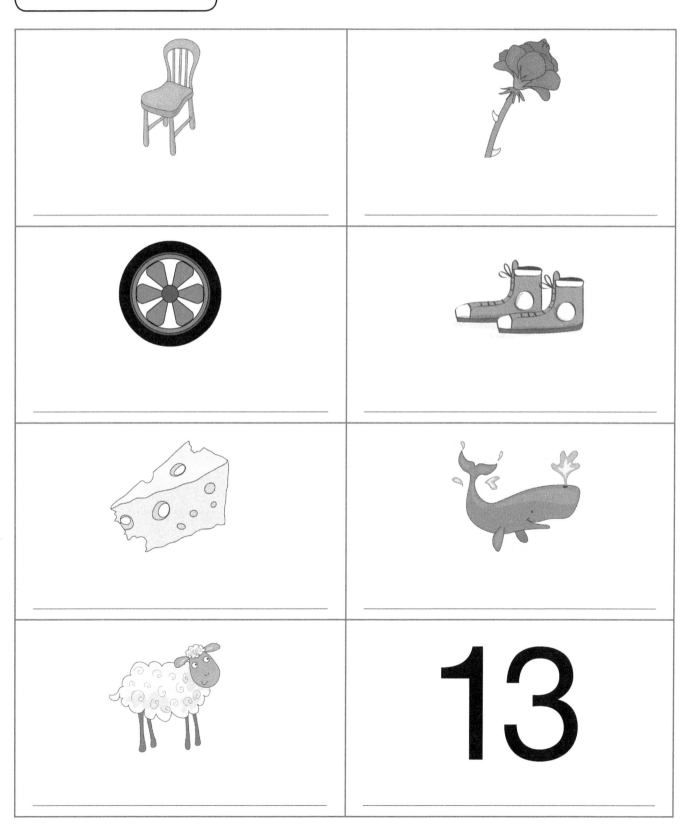

End of unit assessment

Read the instructions below.

1 Cut along the dotted lines.

2 Put the sentences in the correct order.

3 Read and check that the story makes sense.

4 Stick the sentences in the correct order onto paper.

5 Read and check.

✂

Max got a ladder.

Max went to swim in a deep pool. Then …

Max got Bee back to the ground.

Bee got stuck up a small tree.

Phonics *ng*

1 Write the correct word for each picture.

2 Use the letters to make rhyming words.

s k	h r	l s
ring	bang	dong

Phonics *ck*

❶ Write the correct word for each picture.

❷ Use the letters to make rhyming words.

| k   l | d   s | d   l |

pick   lock   suck

_____   _____   _____

_____   _____   _____

End of unit assessment

Label the picture of the tiger. Use the words in the box.

| paws | tail | stripes | nose | teeth | ears | eyes |

Phonics – adjacent consonants at the end of words

1 Circle the correct word ending. Write the words.

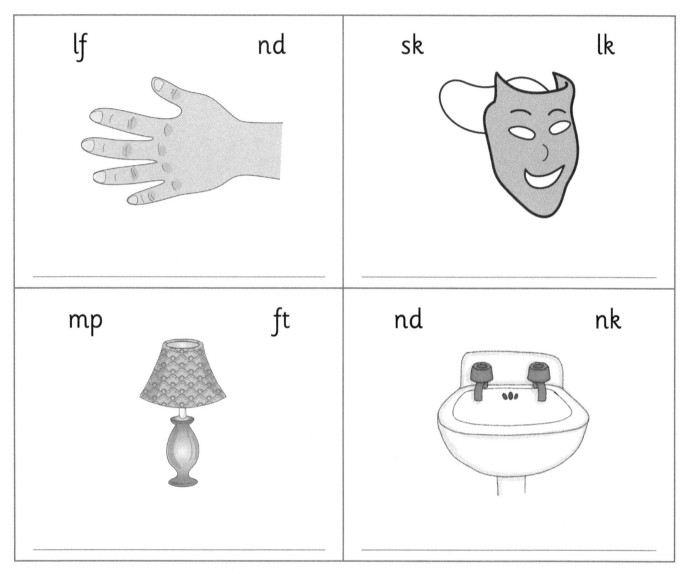

| lf | nd | sk | lk |

_____

_____

| mp | ft | nd | nk |

_____

_____

2 Use the letters to make rhyming words.

| j   p | | b   s | | m   b |

bump

land

send

_____

_____

_____

_____

_____

_____

Phonics – adjacent consonants at the beginning of words

❶ Circle the correct word beginning. Write the words.

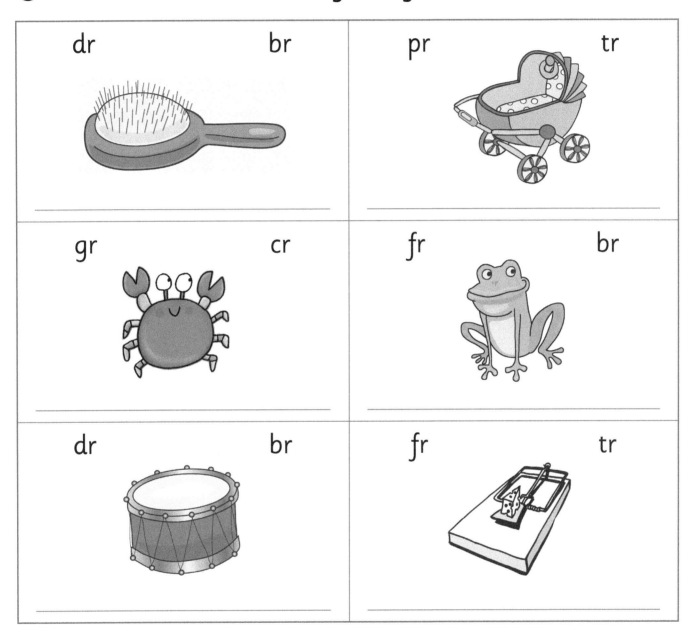

dr br	pr tr
gr cr	fr br
dr br	fr tr

❷ Complete the sentences.

- Dan plays the _____ in the band.

- The _____ hid in the grass.

- The _____ is on the rock.

✓

Phonics – adjacent consonants at the beginning of words

❶ Tick the correct word for each picture. Write the words.

swim ☐ swell ☐   skid ☐ skip ☐

_____   _____

swing ☐ swim ☐   stem ☐ step ☐

_____   _____

❷ Complete the sentences.

- Zenib will stand on the top _____.

- Tim likes to _____ on the grass.

- Fran can _____ well.

Phonics – adjacent consonants at the beginning of words

Match the pictures with the words. Write the words.

trap _____

plug _____

flag _____

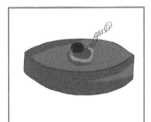

clock _____

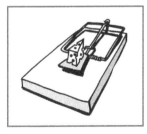

slug _____

glasses _____

End of unit assessment

Complete and copy these sentences.

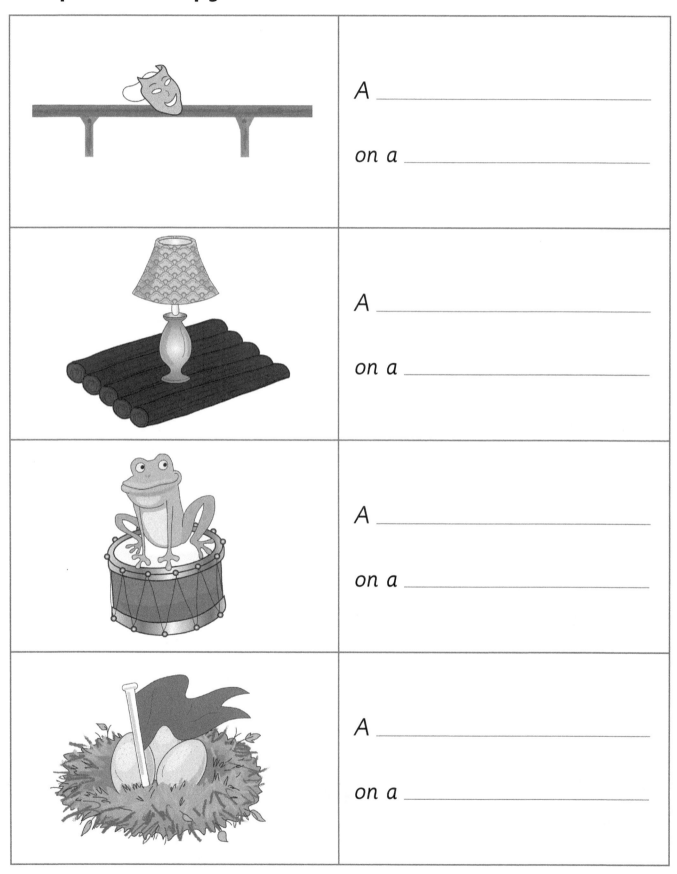

A _____

on a _____

A _____

on a _____

A _____

on a _____

A _____

on a _____

End of unit assessment

Read the poem. Write pairs of rhyming words.

Nut Tree

Small, brown, hard, round,
The nut is lying underground.

Now a shoot begins to show,
Now the shoot begins to grow.

Tall, taller, tall as can be,
The shoot is growing into a tree.

And branches grow and stretch and spread
With twigs and leaves above your head.

And on a windy day
The nut tree bends, the branches sway.

The leaves fly off and whirl around,
And nuts go tumbling to the ground.
Small, brown, hard and round.

By Julia Donaldson

_____   _____

_____   _____

_____   _____

_____   _____

End of unit assessment

Match the foods with their food group

Fruit and vegetables

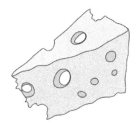

Bread and cereal

Fish and seafood

Dairy and eggs

Phonics *ee*

❶ Write the correct word for each picture.

❷ Complete the sentences.

- The _____ are lost on the hill.

- The _____ stung my leg.

- The nest is in the _____.

- I brush my _____ at night.

Phonics *oa*

❶ Write the word to name each picture.

_____   _____   _____

❷ Use the letters to make rhyming words.

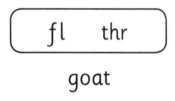

| fl   thr |
goat

| t   r |
coast

_____   _____

_____   _____

❸ Complete the sentences.

- Joan had _____ and jam.

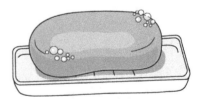

- The _____ fell in the sink.

- Krisha has a hood on her _____ .

Phonics *ai*

1 Write the word to name each picture.

2 Write the three words that rhyme in question 1.

_____ _____ _____

3 Write words that rhyme with 'pail'.
   Use the letters in the box to help.

| f   j   r   s   t |

_____ _____ _____

_____ _____ _____

End of unit assessment

Write a sentence to tell what happened in each picture.

	_____ _____ _____
	_____ _____
	_____ _____
	_____ _____ _____
	_____ _____

Words ending in –ed and –ing

Complete the table. Use the endings –ed and –ing.
One has been done for you.

lick	licked	licking
grunt		
melt		
land		
dust		
print		
rest		
shift		

Phonics *oo*

❶ Write the word to name each picture.

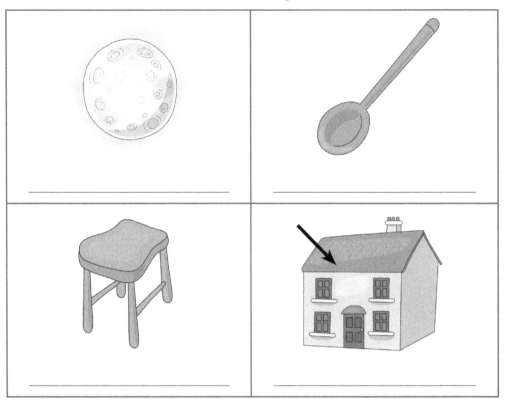

❷ Complete the sentences.

- The cat is on the _____ .

- The _____ is in the pot.

- Josh sat on the _____ .

❸ Use the letters to make rhyming words.

m s		r sh		gr br

noon   boot   room

_____   _____   _____

_____   _____   _____

End of unit assessment

Write the word to name each picture.

Phonics *ie*

1 Write the words to name each picture.

2 Complete the sentences.

- Ben had a stain on his _____.

- The _____ was too hot to cut.

- Do not let _____ land on the food.

3 Use the letters to make rhyming words.

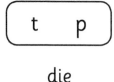   cr   tr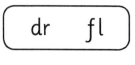

die   tied   cries

_____   _____   _____

_____   _____   _____

End of unit assessment

❶ Complete the sentences.

The servants saw the _____ – in the _____.

"I will catch it with _____ net," said Crumb.

"Then I will tie it up with _____," said Grim.

❷ Write what happened next.

_____

_____

Text acknowledgements

The publishers gratefully acknowledge the permissions granted to reproduce copyright material in the book. Every effort has been made to contact the holders of copyright material, but if any have been inadvertently overlooked, the Publisher will be pleased to make the necessary arrangements at the first opportunity.

HarperCollins Publishers Ltd for an extract and artwork from *The Big Red Bus* by Alison Hawes, illustrated by Woody Fox, text copyright © Alison Hawes, 2006; artwork from *Let's Go Shopping*, illustrated by Jamie Oliver; artwork from *Best Bird* by Laura Hambleton, copyright © Laura Hambleton, 2005; an extract and artwork from *Max Can Do It* by Charlotte Raby, illustrated by Sam Hearn, text copyright © Charlotte Raby, 2011; artwork reproduced by permission of HarperCollins Publishers; Plum Pudding Illustration Agency. HarperCollins Publishers for an extract from *Animal Coats* by Clare Llewellyn, copyright © Clare Llewellyn, 2011; an extract from *In the Forest* by Becca Heddle, copyright © Becca Heddle, 2011; an extract and artwork from *Bot on the Moon*, by Shoo Rayner, copyright © Shoo Rayner; an extract and artwork from *Funny Fish* by Michaela Morgan, illustrated by Jon Stuart, text copyright © Michaela Morgan; an extract from *The Small Bun* by Martin Waddell, illustrated by T. S. Spookytooth, text copyright © Martin Waddell. Text reproduced by permission of HarperCollins Publishers; David Higham Associates; artwork reproduced by permission of HarperCollins Publishers Ltd; Illustration Web. HarperCollins Publishers Ltd for an extract and artwork from *The Lonely Penguin*, written and illustrated by Petr Horacek, copyright © Petr Horacek; an extract and artwork from *Catching the Moon* by Mal and Elspeth Graham, illustrated by Xiao Xin, text copyright © Mal and Elspeth Graham. Artwork reproduced by permission of HarperCollins Publishers Ltd; Illustration Web.

We are grateful to Julia Donaldson for the poem 'The Nut Tree' published in *The Gruffalo's Child Song and Other Songs*, 2012, Macmillan Children's, © Julia Donaldson.